# Good Practice in Supervision with Psychotherapists and Counsellors

# Dedication

To Jeanne, a close, accurate and stimulating reader.
This book is also dedicated to my supervisees and my supervisors, from whom I have learned much.
A special word of thanks must also go to the contributors of 'Reflections'. I am very grateful to them for their support.

# Good Practice in Supervision with Psychotherapists and Counsellors

## The Relational Approach

### DON FEASEY MA

Psychoanalytic Psychotherapist

W
WHURR PUBLISHERS
LONDON AND PHILADELPHIA

© 2002 Whurr Publishers

First published 2002 by
Whurr Publishers Ltd
19b Compton Terrace, London N1 2UN, England and
325 Chestnut Street, Philadelphia PA19106, USA

**British Library Cataloguing in Publication Data**

A catalogue record for this book is available from the
British Library.

ISBN  1 86156 303 5

Printed and bound in the UK by Athenaeum Press Limited,
Gateshead, Tyne & Wear.

# Contents

# Preface

In approaching the task of writing this book I had to take a decision about where I wanted to place myself as the author. I could have decided to emphasize a scholarly, research-based approach to the subject and trawled the publications, books and journals to produce a book that would no doubt be of value to teachers within an academic context. This is a worthwhile activity. Coming from a background of university, polytechnic and college teaching, I know and respect the work of research-based publications.

But I chose not to go in that direction. My reasons are quite straightforward. I wanted to use my own experience of twenty years as a psychotherapist and supervisor to support the advocacy of a particular approach to supervision which I feel is currently under threat. Perhaps this word is too strong. The threat is not intended but is the outcome of academic input into a realm of psychotherapy and counselling supervision. The world of psychotherapy and counselling has traditionally espoused its own culture of training. That culture has come down through time from the powerful teachings of Freud and other analytic schools to the writing and practice of Carl Rogers. It is primarily focussed upon the nature and quality of interpersonal relationships and the internal life of the individual. In this respect, it is deeply subjective.

My view is that the relational approach to the practice and theory of supervision produces good work, but it is not particularly susceptible to research approaches that spring from an academic tradition, where the emphasis is upon measurable objective material.

For example, it is fairly easy to get a research response from therapists to a simple question asking them to report whether they felt nervous in their first encounter with a supervisor. This kind of question may often be put; and from it may be elicited a quantifiable table from which certain deductions may be made. What is much more difficult to obtain, through this research-based approach, is knowledge of the subjective character of the 'nervousness' and its origins and meaning in a relationship.

The result in this book is that I am often thrown back upon my own authority derived from long experience and interest in the subject of supervision. And so my readers will have to take some of what I write on trust. No doubt they will judge for themselves.

I do, however, where appropriate, draw the attention of readers to writers and publications that I have personally found useful. This selection is obviously partial but will provide readers with helpful guidance if they should wish to proceed further with their enquiries.

In sympathy with this approach I have adopted an informal style of writing, using personal, anecdotal vignettes to illustrate points I am making in the text. I have also done my best to render all the people mentioned in these short accounts as anonymous as possible; so names, times, places and sometimes genders have all been changed. Without the experience of their presence this book could not have been written.

**Don Feasey, 2001**

# Introduction
# Good practice in supervision with psychotherapists and counsellors:

## The relational approach

*Please note I use the terms **therapist**, **psychotherapist**, **counsellor** and **creative therapist** throughout this book in the following way: **therapist** is used as a generic term to include all persons and disciplines of therapy and counselling, **psychotherapist** is restricted to those who would normally describe themselves that way, many of them are registered as such with the UKCP, **counsellor** indicates those who describe themselves that way and are for the most part registered with the BACP and **creative therapist** is a generic term covering those who work as psychodramatists and dramatherapists. These are usually registered with a professional body.*

For the past twenty years I have been working as a psychotherapist in private practice and for a dozen of those years as a sessional principal psychotherapist in an NHS mental hospital in the north of England. In my role as a psychotherapist I have given much time to the provision of supervision for trainee psychotherapists, for those working as ancillary workers alongside therapists and for fully mature and qualified psychotherapists in public and private practice. In addition I have always had a small but valued group of senior counsellors who have employed me as a private supervisor for their own private practice. I have also provided supervision to dramatherapists and psychodramatists within a training and working context.

For the most part the supervision has been offered individually, but from time to time I have organised and run supervision groups, which has proved a useful and innovative way of working.

I now regard this aspect of my work to be as important as my direct clinical work with clients; it provides challenge, satisfaction and enduring professional relationships, which have a completely different flavour from that experienced in clinical practice. Furthermore, it provides income at quite a generous level, an important aspect for private practitioners like myself.

It is from this experience that I have set out to write this book, which I hope will prove useful to supervisors and their clients, whatever therapeutic discipline they come from. It is interesting that, although different schools of counselling and psychotherapy would find it difficult to accept the supervisory constructs of each other's ideology, they virtually all see supervision as central to their training and professional practice. So concept and content are very different, and in this book I try not to advance one exclusive form of supervision as superior to another in a comparative and rivalrous manner. However, it will be clear that I do have a value system of my own, which will become quite evident when I write about supervision and its place in therapy and counselling.

The book is intended to be a professional working document offering insights into the nature of supervision as a concept and as a working method. It intends to offer guidance to psychotherapists and counsellors who share, as an almost unique aspect of their profession, the roles of supervisee and supervisor within the same professional life space. For many counsellors and therapists it is simply a natural progression to the role of supervisor that comes about with time and experience. In this respect the profession of counsellor or therapist is probably unique. Largely, the progress towards the role of supervisor has been through experiential learning in the mutual exchange between supervisor and supervisee. I shall have much more to say about this at a later point in this book.

It is true that other forms of supervision exist, within a managerial context, and are practised in other professions and that this can sometimes cause confusion, especially when they occur in clinical settings such as hospitals or in the training of nurses, doctors and paramedics. This confusion will be addressed and discussed and shown to be not of the character of supervision in psychotherapy and counselling.

The concept of supervision has existed in the world of work and learning, especially the learning of skills and tasks in industry and agriculture, for as long as the recorded history of work has existed. So psychotherapy cannot claim the idea of supervision as being specific and exclusive to itself. But what is special about supervision in therapy is the manner in which the concept has been integrated into the continuing practice of psychotherapy and counselling, from the earliest experience of the beginning learner struggling with their first clients right through to the most experienced and well-qualified practitioner managing a stable caseload.

Traditionally, supervision in industry, commerce and trade has been based upon a hierarchical model where the supervisor is the holder of skills, knowledge and information and the supervisee is the learner who defers to the higher position of the supervisor. It relates to the apprentice form of training and learning where the trainee stands close to the practice of the expert and, in the process, learns the trade. This at first seems a long way from the learning process of psychotherapy, but in reality the supervisor of psychotherapy and counselling trainees is frequently a long-established, skilled psychotherapist or counsellor who meets regularly with the trainee to take part in a learning dialogue where inevitably the supervisor is going to carry a good deal of authoritative weight, which the trainee ignores at her peril. Again, this feature of the process and the accompanying roles will get more attention later in this book.

The situation in the supervision of established, well-qualified, practising therapists is rather different. The supervisor and therapist are close to one another in skills, knowledge and experience. However, the work of the supervisor in such a situation is of a more subtle character, and the dialogue is more equal and professionally level. In this situation the supervisor is providing a professional experience, standing, metaphorically speaking, at a distance from the therapist and yet, paradoxically, with the therapist in the therapy situation. This is a stance that is lodged in the culture of therapy and is concerned with enabling the therapist to address subjective intrapsychic as well as interpersonal issues. The emphasis of the dialogue will probably be placed upon the feelings and emotional experience of the therapist, in respect of her relationship with her client. This will include the worlds of fantasy and reality, feeling and thought, imagination and knowing in the world, within the therapeutic dialogue, and the realities of the world outside the consulting room.

For the trainee psychotherapist much will be the same but perhaps with a stronger emphasis upon the presence of transference and countertransference within the relationship with the presented client. Certain technical features of the work may come into focus, such as the presence and effect of 'defence mechanisms' and the place of 'interpretation' in the examined session.

For the trainee counsellor a strong feature of supervision is the giving of emotional support in the supervision relationship. The supervisor is very much a mentor and model for the counsellor in training. She models empathic attention and the ability to offer insightful reflection as well as to inculcate the values of the counselling code.

When the work is with creative therapists, there will be other, but no less important, technical features to address. In Chapter 9 I discuss this situation with more attention and detail.

The academic world has for a long time had its own form and use of supervision. It operates largely within the postgraduate level of learning, where the candidate for a higher degree is required to compose and submit an advanced dissertation that will have to be defended. Very often the higher degree, which is being supervised for its content and method, will have come as an addendum to at least three years of undergraduate learning leading to the first degree. The student in this situation is placed in a very dependent position in regard to their relationship with the supervisor. Beyond the supervisor there also looms the shadowy figure of the 'expert' external examiner. I can still remember quite vividly the day I was to confront the external examiner for my higher degree dissertation, which I thought I might have to defend against astringent criticism. I dreaded the occasion. I need not have worried. The external examiner turned out to be a 'radical' young lecturer in literature from Essex University, regarded in those days as a hotbed of radicalism in both political and academic settings. I knew him only by name, but I felt a comfortable identification with him. It need not have been so.

This position still applies in most respects today. The world of academic practice is slow to change. As for psychotherapy and counselling training courses, the idea of the trainees having to 'defend' a dissertation would be a strange one. Trainees might well find themselves discussing a case study with an external visitor to their training course, but the atmosphere is unlikely to be confrontational.

It is interesting to watch how certain practices in the academic field are subject to strain and stress as more and more courses in psychotherapy and counselling are being offered within academic institutions of one kind or another. Of course, the interplay is in both directions and trainers in academic settings are subject to the expectations of their promoting institutions.

This situation will be addressed again in Chapter 1 of this book, where I discuss the origins of supervision and relate the topic to situations, structures and employment other than psychotherapy and counselling.

Supervision is often thought of as being in the possession of either employers or trainers. But there is a healthy presence of supervision in private practice that caters mainly for private counsellors and psychotherapists and sometimes, if rarely, those employed but encouraged by their employers to find supervision in the private sector.

The supervisor in such a situation, who is placed outside the therapist's employment situation, may well be called upon to address employment issues and the context of therapy practice. This would include all issues that affect the practice of therapy, whether of a management character or vested in issues of accommodation, infrastructure, support and so on. The following example illustrates an extreme and demanding situation that arose because of the confusion within an organisation (a large hospital) about the role of a creative therapist and the professional guidelines that she worked towards, which constituted guidance for her in practice and the supervision dialogue.

## Example

*A woman client, a creative therapist working full time in a hospital setting, came to me monthly for clinical supervision. This was an agreed arrangement with her hospital manager, and the supervision fees were refunded to her on production of a receipt from myself.*

*One morning, in her office, preparing for a creative therapy session with a group of patients, she received a telephone call from a very senior nurse administrator instructing her to go to a ward to cover the absence of a competent member of the nursing staff.*

*Two issues immediately came to the therapist's mind. The first was her commitment to the creative-therapy group, which was well established and where there would be consternation if she simply sent them a message saying she could not attend. The second issue was the more pressing. The ward she was being asked to cover was a ward for severely disturbed patients, all of them receiving medication. My client felt she was not qualified or competent to replace a charge nurse and to take charge of the ward with all its clinical responsibilities. The implications were frightening. My client refused to obey the nurse administrator's instructions. The consequences for her were considerable.*

The reader will probably immediately see that profound professional issues were raised in this example. Dealing with the many-layered problems that arose in this situation proved to be testing for the therapist and supervisor alike. More will be discussed in relation to this case in Chapter 3.

Readers will become aware that I am advocating a relational approach to supervision for psychotherapists and counsellors. I have been prompted to address this issue directly because there is now appearing a movement towards the training of supervisors that suggests a didactic approach to their training. I certainly have no objection to people being urged to *think* about the training process of supervisors, but I am concerned that the thinking process might come to dominate the procedure of training at the expense of feeling, and reflecting upon, the whole relationship of supervisor and supervisee.

A recent book, *Group Supervision: A Guide to Creative Practice* (2000), puts the position clearly. The author, Brigid Proctor, a professional trainer, writes, from page 13 onwards, an outline of what she calls a 'theoretical orientation' and quotes Carroll (1996), who describes supervision as moving steadily towards models of supervision based on social roles, developmental stages and so on. Carroll notes that writers on supervision are moving away from what he describes as 'counselling-bound' approaches and this could easily include 'psychotherapy-bound' approaches. The implication is that the world of training in supervision is trying to move the focus towards a structured model of learning theory. This is essentially an academic model and is familiar to educators. Brigid Proctor's book is a clear example of this movement, and one cannot do anything except admire its display of reasoning and application. Her book attempts to place the didactic approach to supervision alongside what she describes as the 'Group Supervision Alliance Model'. Her aim seems to be to hold on to the experiential component of learning, thus the suggestion of 'creativity' in her title. Readers will judge as to how far she succeeds.

But *this* book, *Good Practice in Supervision With Psychotherapists And Counsellors: The Relational Approach*, takes the reader in an entirely different direction, embedding the theory and practice of supervision firmly within its therapeutic origins; a relationship where, I believe, it belongs.

The relational approach to the supervision of counsellors and psychotherapists insists that supervision, like therapy, is owned by the world of psychotherapy and counselling and is an outgrowth of its special and particular culture. That is the position of my argument.

Douglas Fraser, in 'Reflections' at the end of this book, makes a telling point when he removes the prefix 'super-' from the word 'supervision' and leaves us with the emphatic statement 'vision'. The idea of 'vision' is central to the relational approach, implying as it does the presence of emotional energy in the work of the supervisee and supervisor together.

*Indeed, if I were asked to state briefly the aim of this book I would reply: 'I hope it gives the reader something to think and feel about.'*

A small, technical point: the persona in academic texts is often portrayed as male. We are accustomed to reading 'he said this' or 'he said that'. Also, it seems that the collective 'we' of the text is assumed to be male.

In this book I am reversing the practice and my persona is female. I am doing this as a small gesture of recognition that for the most part counsellors and psychotherapists are female, and the trend is increasingly going that way. It should be recognized.

# Chapter 1
# The origins of supervision

'Supervision of Psychotherapy; is it Teaching? Is it Administration? Is it Therapy?'

(Ekstein, in Holloway, 1995, p. 4)

Jon Rowan defines supervision as 'A passionate joint enquiry'.

(quoted in Inskipp and Proctor, 1995)

**The Final Supervision**

When the board was set to play,
There was the chessmaster and the pawn.

'What is it you wish of me?' queried the chessmaster.
'To help me become a knight, ' answered the pawn.
'And why are you not already what you wish?' asked the chessmaster.
'I have no armour, no sword and no horse,' said the pawn.
'And you wish that I should provide that for you?' demanded the chessmaster.
'Oh, no, not that,' replied the faltering pawn. 'I wish only that you show me the means by which they may be acquired.'
'Agreed,' responded the chessmaster.

Karen A. Pirnot
University of Iowa

'The process of supervision, like all human relationships, is fraught with hazards' (Rioch, 1980, p. 69).

This chapter is concerned with a *brief* examination of the origins of the idea of supervision, its roots in work and the relationship of the worker to her mentor: the supervisor. It is true that many forms of supervision exist and are practised in other professions and trades and that this can sometimes cause confusion to those examining supervision in the counselling and psychotherapy process.

This confusion, which centres mainly upon the issue of power and authority, judgement and assessment, will be addressed and discussed in this book and shown to be not of the character of supervision in psychotherapy

1

and counselling. As I have suggested in the Introduction, the concept of supervision has existed in the world of work and learning, especially the learning of skills and tasks, for as long as the recorded history of work has existed. So psychotherapy cannot claim the idea of supervision as being specific and exclusive to itself.

The special character of supervision in therapy lies in the relationship of the supervisor and the supervisee. It is this relationship that, I argue, conditions the nature of the supervision experience for both parties. At its best it supports a creative and positive experience of mutual learning, at its worst it supports varying forms of abuse. (See Sue Kaberry's chapter on abuse in supervision in Lawton and Feltham, 2000.) There is also the danger that this powerful history of supervision practice, originating in psychoanalysis and operating today in virtually all forms of therapy and counselling, brings with it what Proctor (2000) describes as the 'closed system'. By this she means where current practices are based almost exclusively on past practice, passed down from generation to generation, ensuring a guardianship of past practice that puts it beyond reproach, examination or change. Let God forbid! My belief is that the approach I am advocating in this book will protect the practice from such fossilisation while at the same time acknowledging its threat.

In supervision in industry the apprentice stands beside the expert and in the process learns the trade. The apprentice witnesses the expert in action. In therapy supervision the supervisor is frequently a long-established, skilled psychotherapist or counsellor, who meets regularly with the trainee to take part in a learning dialogue, where inevitably the supervisor is going to be experienced as an expert, or so it may seem. But the supervisor is not seen in action by the trainee and, significantly, neither does the supervisor see the supervisee in action.

Two years of working in a factory that had a strong craft element in its manufacturing process took me close to the master craftsman–apprentice form of learning and the intense social and psychological elements of that experience for those concerned. There seemed to be three positions for the relationship, not exclusive but very influential, each one feeding into the others:

- the position of *idealization*
- the *instrumental* position
- the *dependency* position.

I was quick to respond to these positions in my work as a progress chaser in the factory. The factory produced woodwork for new houses, which was a completely contemporary, industrialized activity. It provided for the vast expansion of council housing that was a feature of post-war Britain. In addition it also provided a highly skilled craft service of ecclesiastical joinery, sculpture and metal work, the origins of which went back hundreds of years. The worker populations could hardly have been more contrasted.

The first position, *idealization*, most evident in the craft section of the factory, was where the craftsman seemed to carry all the best aspects of the trade he practised. And this was not only the skills element of the trade but also its historical values and culture. So, as an example, a wood carver practising his trade in a workshop at the factory would have a distinct framework of cultural reference, historical in character, going back many hundreds of years, relating to his trade that marked him out from the stonemason and metalworker and kept him at a vast distance from the ordinary wood joiner on the factory floor. The apprentice attached to the wood carver, by contract, for a good number of years, would soon assimilate these values and perspectives, which would have the effect of consolidating his apprenticeship relationship and keeping him firmly attached to the craftsman as an idealized figure.

## Example

*Many years ago I went regularly to Harry the hairdresser who was a renowned medal winner in competitions. He was an agreeable, laid-back character, friendly and attentive to the needs of his clients, old or young, children or adult males. He had a string of young female apprentices, all of them learning to 'cut' with expertise and ease as well as developing a 'chairside' manner modelled on Harry. What struck me was the passivity of the young women; they appeared content to wash up mugs, brush up the hair and keep the floor and working surfaces spotlessly clean. When not doing this they simply stood and watched intently as Harry worked on the customer and conducted a pleasant conversation, often based on what he knew of the customer. He regularly took the apprentices to shows and competitions, even going abroad, where they were chaperoned by their mothers. Harry was idealized to an amazing degree, but he seemed remarkably unaffected by it in any unpleasant or egotistical manner.*

It seems to me that part of the process of *idealization* of the skilled craftsman by the apprentice is the attractive idea that the apprentice will, one day, enjoy such idealization and move into the aristocracy of the highly skilled. Interestingly enough, in the factory described, money did not spell out membership of this élite. Indeed, I was very shocked when I discovered how little they were paid. Their superior position was maintained by the level of their expertise, by the relative scarcity of their skilled labour and by the long training period apprentices had to serve to join the ranks of this privileged group. Their standing was entirely based on skills that were centuries old.

The second position I would describe as *instrumental*. In other words, the relationship between the craftsman and the apprentice was based on necessity. It was essentially utilitarian. The apprentice was contracted by the employer to enter into the apprenticeship and then allocated to a craftsman whose job it was to inculcate the skills and knowledge of that particular trade. This does not rule out an idealized component in the relationship but rather the utilitarian aspect stands in the background of the work experience and is known to all parties as the apprenticeship agreement. To achieve the necessary level of skills to enter the 'trade' was an imperative in the relationship with the master craftsman. The skills themselves were built upon hundreds of years of repeated practice, leaving only very limited room for personal variation.

Some of the skill was knowledge based. The apprentice would learn to recognize certain woods, metals or pieces of stone, where these materials came from, what they were best used for, how they should be stored and, finally, chosen to be manipulated by skilful hands, through the use of special tools, to achieve a proper outcome. The other level of learning was in the use of the hands, eye and mind in the performance of the task. There was much 'social learning' to be accomplished as well.

*Dependency*, the third position, again not exclusively or solely present, is the situation of prolonged infantilization experienced by the apprentice and the corresponding and matching experience of parenthood on the part of the tradesman: a mutually dependent relationship. For the most part in the factory where I worked it was a case of father and son. The apprentices were for the most part about fifteen and sixteen years old. They were in the grip of adolescence. What supported and sustained them in this usually demanding period of their lives was their position in the workshops. They knew they were destined to be adult and 'superior'. They had no need to fight and struggle with their craft fathers to gain such a position. On the contrary, they were there to learn, emulate and eventually to gain the benefit of craft status.

I was intrigued by the situation in the stained-glass department, where the apprentice was a good-looking girl, who did her best to present as a slim male youth. Anorexia was unknown to me then, but I think she was probably in the grip of that condition, playing the clever, attractive son to her craftsman/artist father in the workshop. This is only a guess, many years after the event, but certainly her position of deference to the master stained-glass maker was evident, as was her own developing expertise, which I admired.

Lastly, I would mention the use of the term 'supervisor' in relation to authority, emphasized in certain work situations.

## Example

*As a student, many years ago, working in a holiday job for the then British Railways Accounts Office, I was placed under the supervision of a senior office worker. She was not so senior as to be regarded as a manager, but had enough experience, maturity and ability to supervise my work in a direct, judgmental manner. In other words, I was required to satisfy her that I was doing a good job. She was someone to whom I could turn for information and support. Nevertheless, she was in a clear position of authority and my well-being depended to some extent on her approval. Most workers will evaluate themselves to some extent by the standards of their supervisor and the status of the supervisor in the pecking order of the working context. The higher the status of the supervisor, the more satisfaction is likely to be felt by the supervisee.*

*I felt this quite intensely when, although in what was a holiday job, I was promoted to the position of depot tracer, a job with considerable responsibility involving the search for lost goods of all kinds in transit on the railway. My supervisor was no longer a relatively humble shopfloor worker but the chief accountant himself. This was the man who had promoted me in the first place, but no doubt my first supervisor had had her say in the matter.*

This definition of supervisor and supervision is common in business and industry – where there is no strong craft tradition and the skills, while important, are acquired quickly – and is clearly a long way from what I have described above, and even further from the meaning of the term in counselling and psychotherapy.

It can be quickly seen from the descriptions given that there are elements of similar experience that match that of counsellors and psychotherapists in training. The culture of training in both counselling and psychotherapy encourages regression in the trainees. The training, too, occupies relatively long periods of attachment to the training experience, in a relatively junior position of institutional membership, and is the path that leads to eventual full membership of that training organization. It might be described as the path from childhood to maturity, as an adult. Again the 'adult' psychotherapy and counselling position is highly valued within its culture.

There is, frequently, a value system and a specific culture embedded in the history of the training body or bodies that the trainee encounters. For example, both my own validating institute and the nearest institute to me geographically have their roots in NHS practice, and this is detectable in their current ideology of training and practice. Most trainees incorporate the culture and value system without much questioning, sometimes with unfortunate results (Masson, 1992). This seems to me inevitable and needs to be regarded as a fact of life rather than as a tendency to be constantly challenged, either from inside or outside the organization concerned. Rather, what I am advocating is that in approaching and dealing with psychotherapy training bodies and their counterparts in the counselling world one would be well advised to take into account the cultural filter that surrounds each and every one of them.

I have already touched on the matter of supervision in the academic world in the Introduction. It operates largely within the postgraduate level of learning, where the candidate, for a higher degree, is required to compose and submit an advanced dissertation that will have to be defended.

For the most part the student is in her postgraduate phase and to some extent has passed through the most 'dependent' aspect of her learning process, as experienced in the undergraduate position. She may not yet be fully mature as a person, or as an academic, but she will have acquired knowledge and skill as a learner in those earlier years. She will have enjoyed enough success and approval to encourage her to move forward in her academic progress.

The supervisor will probably have been appointed or selected as a result of being a 'specialist' in the area of study chosen by the postgraduate student.

So from the beginning a hierarchy of learning is established. The supervisor is the 'expert', and the 'postgrad' is the learner. Here are echoes of the apprenticeship position. This relationship may persist for a long time, especially if the student proceeds to a doctorate level of study, which can easily continue for another five years. It could be argued that these supervisory years are essentially transitory years as admission to the academic profession proceeds. It is common for PhD students to teach in the university, albeit on the level of introductory courses that their 'betters' do not wish to be bothered with.

Although both counselling and psychotherapy learning incorporate some academic content, they present themselves very differently to the trainee. Psychoanalysis, in particular, has an important and vast library of theory, some of it highly disputatious, arising from years of theoretical speculation, discussion, argument, research and revision. There is no agreed common body of knowledge in psychoanalytic studies; although there are many overlapping areas of theoretical 'agreement' between the different psychoanalytic institutes, there are as many points of deep disagreement. I find it interesting, too, how a relatively new subject has appeared in university studies called 'counselling psychology', which is clearly aimed at lifting the theories of counselling into an academic context of research and teaching. It will eventually impact on counsellor training. This development may well give rise to other theories to rival it. We shall have to wait and see.

Formal academic and clinical psychology, too, is slowly adapting to the presence of psychoanalytical-psychotherapy theory and person-centred teaching and, in turn, is beginning to produce a responsive literature.

Many of the newer breed of counsellors and psychotherapists will have qualified at the level of an MA course, in which role they may have experienced the academic supervision I have described. They may have imbibed an approach that is not at all compatible with therapeutic supervision and repeat it when they in turn, with the passing of time, become supervisors to therapists and counsellors. The intellectualization of psychotherapy and counselling studies continues without abating and sometimes seems to threaten the experiential component of therapy training. On occasions it is almost as if the training bodies turn away from the difficulties of measuring and adjudicating the deeply subjective issues of experiential learning, central though these issues may be to the good practice of counselling and therapy.

**Example**

*Robert came to me for his clinical-work supervision when he enrolled for a course in integrative psychotherapy. Very little effort was made to contact me by his training body to check out my theoretical position regarding compatibility with their training ideology. Indeed, several years later, when he completed the course, with distinction, no account appeared to be taken of the clinical work he had pursued in relation to his training. I was not contacted; I was surprised.*

This stands in strong contrast to the training of many psychoanalysts who are reported upon by their supervisors, during their training, to their psychoanalytical institute providers. The impact of such practice on the relationship of supervisor/supervisee seems to me deeply problematic. I can imagine many counsellors and therapists in training would shrink from such an arrangement. I have quite often come across supervisors working with trainee counsellors also functioning as tutors on the same course. I imagine this sets up tensions from time to time as roles become confused.

I have had experience of two institutes that seem unwilling to trust the supervision of trainees to anyone except those who are members of their organization: those who have received their direct 'blessing' for the task to be performed. Where is the independence of the supervisor then, one might ask? It seemed in both cases that membership of the UKCP, in the appropriate section, was not good enough for the organizations concerned.

**Example**

*Some years ago a man approached me to ask me to be his training supervisor while he pursued a clinical training course in psychotherapy run by a university in a neighbouring city. After a couple of interviews I agreed, and terms were set out that suited us both and agreed upon. I then suggested to him that he would probably need to clear this arrangement with the course leaders at the university concerned. I did not expect any difficulty. I knew about the training course. It had a good reputation. I knew one of the professors associated with the course, a distinguished person in the field of psychotherapy. I knew too that our theoretical position was close enough not to cause any difficulty. The course was probably more orthodox than I am, inclining towards a Kleinian position, which I certainly do not favour, but not to such an extent as to make super-vision difficult.*

*He submitted my name to the course leaders. They then sent me a formal letter of enquiry and an application form to join their institute. Well I had no wish to join their institute. I had a number of reasons, among which was the matter of the institute fee, which was considerable! The application form astounded me. It wanted to know, in detail, all the relevant facts of my own training and personal therapy and supervision. The fact that I was a registered psychotherapist in the psychoanalytic section of the UKCP did not appear to cut any ice. The fact I was a founding member of one of the largest psychotherapy institutes outside of London did not interest them. I felt annoyed and diminished by their enquiries. 'Who the heck were they to ask these impertinent questions?' I heard myself raging in annoyance. I felt very petulant. I refused to fill in the form and join up. I sent them the statement that I give to clients, which sets out my professional validation. But, regretably, it was not regarded as good enough. So the supervisee and I had to go our separate ways.*

In later chapters I shall come back to these issues again and give them deeper consideration. Suffice for now to recognize that 'supervision' is an arena of complex behaviour and markedly differing opinion and judgements, which gives rise to many variations of practice, some of which bring in their wake conflict and confusion to the work of the supervisor and supervisee alike. I shall be looking, in some detail, at the situation of the supervisor and super-visee working together in relation to a private practice, and I shall be advocating a particular culture of supervision that places emphasis upon the *how* of that professional relationship and the manner in which it might be conducted.

I shall also consider the special issue of counsellors in GP practices where they have to work cheek by jowl with a traditional and conservative medical model, as well as a growing band of counsellors working within clinical psychology departments and, of course, that highly specific area of counselling that is practised in the university sector. Employers of all kinds employ counsellors, either full time or on a consultancy basis, again either directly or through counselling agencies.

What is the specific responsibility of supervisors to counsellors employed in such diverse settings? The rapidly expanding world of counselling services challenges the traditional concepts of counselling and therapy. Notions of boundaries, special techniques and modes of behaviour long valued and preserved by counsellors, therapists and their supervisors are being required to change to accommodate a changing world of employment and mental health care. The context of supervision is being increasingly recognized as critically definitive of the manner of its application (Carroll and Holloway, 1999).

Finally, on a somewhat lighter note, and with a degree of sardonic questioning, I put the suggestive query: should a psychotherapy/counselling supervisor be supervised for the work she is doing in that role? Should the supervisor of the supervisor be supervised? And the supervisor of the supervisor of the supervisor? and so on.

I address this question in my first book (Feasey, 2000) but leave the reader to answer the question herself to her own satisfaction or otherwise.

# Chapter 2
# Supervision in training and organizational clinical practice

It is interesting to note, following the genesis of Freudian psychoanalysis (from its development in the mind, writing and practice of Sigmund Freud to its present-day application), that systematic training in and supervision of psychoanalysis has arrived on the scene only relatively recently. Certainly, with the early debates concerning who should practise psychoanalysis and who should not, the notion of supervision seems hardly to have occurred to anyone. In the early days Freud advanced and developed a defence of psychoanalysis as a practice outside of formal medical training. In 1926 he published the book *The Question of Lay Analysis* in which he defended the right of lay people to work as psychoanalysts, although he insisted that there should be a prior medical referral in certain circumstances.

In America a few years earlier there were outright attacks on lay people working as psychoanalysts, and Dr Abraham Brill, an early admirer of Freud who had supported Freud on his visit to America, called on the Viennese Society to abandon its support of lay analysis in favour of it being a requirement for psychoanalysts to have undergone a medical training. Medical training had its own form and method of supervision, which were clearly lacking in the early psychoanalytical movement. This was an early powerful attempt to 'scientize' and 'medicalize' the practice of psychoanalysis.

For a long time this was a fraught debate. Freud himself seems to have rejected the right of the medical world to acquire for itself an exclusive right to practise psychoanalysis. He insisted upon its broader context of reference, especially in relation to the use of psychoanalytical thinking in the study of history and the humanities. If he had thought of supervision at all, it would have been on quite a different basis – the peer discussion of cases – with a different emphasis than we are accustomed to giving it today.

My own experience as a supervisor has been that only a few of the trainees coming to me have been interested in the broader cultural application of psychoanalytic ideas and theories. Most of them have been thoroughly inculcated, in their training, with a 'clinical', if not medical, model of application of psychotherapy. As a result, much of Freud's non-clinical work and thinking is neglected. Even some of his early work on neuroses, especially that which linked very strongly with interpersonal relationships within the family, is neglected in favour of later thinking, where emphasis has shifted to intrapsychic activity. The idea of psychoanalytic psychotherapy as a 'scientific' procedure is predominant in most training courses.

At the same time there was early voiced concern about the sometimes brief and idiosyncratic path that lay people could take towards acquiring the title 'psychoanalyst'.

Ernest Jones (1957) writes: 'I remember asking Rank, for instance, how he could bring himself to send back to America as a practising analyst someone who had been with him barely six weeks, and he replied with a shrug, "one must live."'

Presumably, the trainee would have returned to America saying he had been analysed by Otto Rank, a man of some distinction in the psychoanalytical movement. The name Rank would have endorsed the new analyst and proved attractive in gaining employment and clients.

Presumably, Rank was only too keen to lay his hand on the desirable 'dollar' currency, as indeed was Freud. Freud writes to Lou Andreas-Salome in 1921, offering to pay her fare to visit him because he has become 'relatively rich in good foreign currency (American, English, Swiss) ... I should like to get some pleasure from my new wealth' (Jones, 1957). It is likely that most of this money came his way through training foreigners in psychoanalysis.

Such a casual attitude would today be insupportable. It is obvious that in those inter-war periods there was no such thing as an institutional control of psychoanalytical training, recognized and enforced on an international basis. Neither was there a presence of systematic supervision of those entering the field of psychoanalytic practice.

In the immediate post-war period there was a relatively slow growth of psychoanalytical training in Britain. What there was came under the auspices of the Institute of Psychoanalysis in London, a body that has always jealously guarded its prerogative in this respect. Gradually the training became more formalized, candidates were scrutinized more closely, but the emphasis was still on personal experience of psychoanalysis by the trainee, which came to be called the training analysis. Training analysts, too, became a special and separate group endowed with the responsibility for inculcating the theories, skills and values of the profession. To become a training analyst was to reach a position where an income was virtually guaranteed and where the holder enjoyed status and power. The training of psychoanalysts was becoming systematized, and in much later years the influence of this training method, with its insistence upon personal therapy, was felt in the broader world of psychotherapy and counselling training.

Its most important influence in the area of supervision is upon the nature of the relationship between the supervisor and the trainee. I shall be dealing with this phenomenon later in this book but even a cursory examination of the situation reveals its complexity and something of its ambiguities. Pedder (1986) puts the old question of to what extent supervision is more than education and less than therapy – a question that is not easily answered. The complexity of the relationship is neatly illustrated by Imre Szecsody (1990). He describes what he calls the 'crowd' in the supervision room: mentor, teacher, evaluator, judge, colleague, friend, confidant and dependant.

To a great extent, the relationship issue is less acute in the history of counsellor training, or appears to be so, and the place of the supervisor in that training has not stirred up so much obvious difficulty of definition. I think this is largely because the issue of transference was not recognized in any significant way, in the early development of counsellor training and practice in the UK. The role of the supervisor took on a more educational, advisory and mentoring position in relation to trainees than in the history of psychoanalytic psychotherapy training. Again, I shall be looking at this more closely in later chapters of this book. Suffice it to say that the experience of supervision in the two therapy strategies of psychotherapy and counselling are somewhat different; although it could be argued that now they are moving closer together as the counselling world takes on board the notion of transference and the unconscious as significant features of the therapeutic relationship. This is frequently referred to as 'psychodynamic counselling theory', which has emerged with some influence in the past ten years. Furthermore, the world of psychoanalytical psychotherapy is beginning to see value in the world of counselling and is less likely, as a result, to be dismissive and disparaging of the practice of counselling. The other place where they stand close together is in the manner in which the supervisee looks for support and understanding, beyond almost everything else in the supervision relationship. This probably applies to every type of training and practice mode of supervision.

We have all come to accept supervision as a required element in therapy training, almost independently of any ideological difference between the therapies. A candidate for any of the major training organizations would expect to have to develop skills, techniques and understanding through clinical practice, and in the process receive supervision from an accredited supervisor, probably appointed by the organization concerned. This would probably be at the candidate's own cost and would run alongside the need for the candidate to receive personal therapy, again from a therapist associated with the organization. The extent to which the clinical practice will be closely or otherwise controlled by the training organization will obviously vary a good deal.

In my own experience as a therapist I have had trainees in my care who were given a wide degree of discretion in the manner of their work with the client. It was assumed, probably in an illusory way, that the supervision process would safeguard the client from any abuse or failure on the part of the trainee. Thus the supervisor carries a high degree of responsibility for the well-being of all concerned. Usually this is not an onerous task, but I have faced situations where I have provoked anxiety in a trainee by insisting upon the trainee taking into account aspects of the therapy that had not been especially examined by his trainers or training organization. For example, I insisted upon the proper recognition of the importance of boundaries and timekeeping and the transference feelings of the client and the trainee when the trainee's own trainers were not, in my view, giving sufficient attention to these matters in their programme of work with the trainee therapists.

I take the view, not always shared by others, that these are fundamental concerns found in any psychotherapy or counselling practice worthy of the name. Sometimes this leads to anxiety and discomfort for the trainee and a sense in myself of becoming a persecutory figure, an experience I did not feel at all comfortable with and one that has to be addressed in the supervision relationship.

Working independently but closely as a supervisor with my own training body, some years ago, I found that I was rarely in dispute, or even feeling uncomfortable, with the main teaching criteria of the trainers. My relationship to the training body was kept clear and delineated by the fact that *I was not required to act as part of the assessment team that eventually declared the trainee fit to be registered with the UKCP as a competent therapist*. The most I am prepared to say about a trainee is that, in my opinion, there is no reason why the trainee should not be professionally registered as a competent therapist. If I felt otherwise, I would hope to address the issues in the supervision sessions.

In a recent edition of *The Psychotherapist* (2000), the journal of the UKCP, Professor Peter Fonagy, Freud Memorial Professor of Psychoanalysis at University College London, is reported as commenting on the unhappy situation in the UK where supervisors of trainees within the psychoanalytical training schools may be required to report on the competence of the trainee to the training organization. He remarks that this will inevitably inhibit the frankness of the supervisee in her relationship with the supervisor. I agree with the professor. At this point it must be acknowledged what a critical feature UKCP registration has been and is increasingly becoming in the development of the training of the contemporary psychotherapist. The UKCP exerts its influence upon individual trainees and qualified therapists by the pressure it can bring to bear on the training bodies. The most recent example of this is the concern that is now being engendered in the training bodies for the concept of continuing professional development. Future supervisors will certainly find they are likely to be drawn into this proposal in one way or another.

The counselling trainees, too, have to watch over their shoulder towards the influence of the British Association for Counselling and Psychotherapy that finally approves their hours of recognized training and counselling experience. The UKCP and the BACP might seem aloof and at a distance from the trainee as she trains, but the reality is that both of these bodies have a profound effect upon training content, style and standards of the trainers. It is the ambition of every newly set up training course to become accredited by the BACP or the UKCP, as the case may be. Even as I write, the UKCP has a standing committee examining the topic of supervision and is probably preparing recommendations that could be enforced within the profession. The reader might have guessed by now I am somewhat sceptical of the value and desirability of the presence of such powerful regulatory bodies. They sit uneasily with the history of psychotherapy. Freedom from regulation provided room for a wide degree of experiment and discovery. If medical regulators had existed powerfully in the late nineteenth century, it is likely that Freud, Breuer, Adler, Jung, Fromm and the rest of the innovators would have been prevented from practising this 'new' therapy that so powerfully challenged the agreed practices of the day. Furthermore, there must be many senior counsellors practising, of my generation, who would fail BACP accreditation if they were challenged today by that body with its present accreditation criteria.

As Fonagy observes, for the most part supervisors working with training organizations are more closely drawn into the influence of the training body than I was. Some even have dual roles working as teachers, with assessment responsibilities, as well as supervisors of trainees' clinical work. This dual-role system, although open to the obvious criticism that conflict of interest may easily occur, is not so rare as it may seem. Balint is quoted by Pedder (1986) as a case of someone who had experienced both the role of therapist and supervisor in the same person. Pedder (1986) himself speaks appreciatively of his own similar experience. I recall that in the 1950s social workers in training at the Tavistock Clinic, in London, were supervised and analysed by the same training therapist. However, there have been important changes in perspective, and the supervisor is now regarded as one who has a special and particular role towards the trainee that is fundamentally different from that of the training therapist. But the issue raised by Pedder and quoted above, concerning the educational aspect of the supervisory role and its therapeutic content, remains something of a tease. Fonagy is reported in the article as stating that Britain is now one of the last remaining countries to support a situation where therapist and supervisor in the training situation also report to the training body as to the suitability and competence of the trainee.

It has to be remembered that virtually all trainees experience some form of therapy or counselling during training, and this can in itself raise questions in the supervision relationship.

### Example

*Ms X was referred to me as a trainee requiring psychoanalytic psychotherapy supervision. She had already acquired a reputation as an extremely clever and argumentative trainee, one who was not slow to dispute with her trainers. She had selected a client for treatment who would thus become the training client and Ms X would in turn become supervised. Unfortunately, her training therapist got involved in an argument about the suitability of the client as a training client and this leaked out into discussion with the trainers. So the boundaries became distorted and argument and disputation spread around the training organization concerning this 'brilliant' but difficult trainee. When she came to me and proposed herself for supervision, I was very aware of the breach of boundary that had occurred between the training therapist and the course trainers in the case of Ms X. My first statement to Ms X was that there would be no further breaches of boundaries, and I would not be in contact, at any time, with her training therapist. We were both relieved at this undertaking. I am pleased to say the course trainers seemed pleased and relieved at my stance.*

Nevertheless, Ms X could not quite prevent herself from bringing the tensions of her relationship with her training therapist to me. Undercurrents of hostility towards the therapist were brought to me somewhat seductively during supervision sessions. She also tended to idealize me and compare me favourably with those, within the institute where she trained, who were teaching her. Transference feelings were very evident and powerful in these supervision sessions. Supervisors would be wise to acknowledge that in this situation it is easy to be sucked into a rivalrous relationship with a training therapist within the same organizational structure. However, it can also happen the other way around.

### Example

*A client, with whom I worked as the training therapist, came to me in great distress concerning her mishandling of the very first training patient she had ever worked with. The problems were largely of a minor technical character, highly inflated by my trainee's anxiety. The trainee was very scared of her supervisor finding out what a bodge she had made of her first meetings with her client. The supervisor was a senior trainer within the organization. So she turned to me for reassurance. My first task was to try to disentangle the fears that lay in the trainee, discovering in herself a potentially uncertain and destructive psychotherapist. And then she had to address the anxiety she felt about being judged as such by her supervisor. Not an easy job. The trainee trusted me completely to keep the boundaries of our relationship, and she was able to express her fears. But she did not trust her supervisor to the same degree. This supervisor had a reputation for being 'tough' and closely identified with the training body. The issue of assessment was never far from her thoughts, even to the extent of fearing she would be found unfit to train as a therapist.*

It is important to recognize that a supervisor working with her own validating institute or organization may well identify with it very positively, in contrast to the what is experienced when working with an organization to which there is no emotional loyalty. We are all human and likely to respond subjectively to institutional pressures according to the way they are perceived, sometimes with warmth, sometimes with hostility.

What is quite clear is that the supervision of trainees within the training establishment will inevitably lead to the confirmation of the guiding ideology of the therapy programme being advanced by the principal trainers. Sometimes that ideology, as in psychoanalysis, is deeply founded in historical experience, carrying with it a succession of powerful training voices that have emerged through the twentieth century. Obviously for psychoanalysis, the rivals to Freud that have emerged, Jung and Klein, carry with them their own special view of the human psyche, and accompanying their theoretical models are appropriate techniques of work. In the counselling world the primacy of Carl Rogers is obvious and I recall, when *On Becoming a Person* (1967) was published, many students, training to work in the helping professions, regarded it as their Bible.

The implications for the trainee are clear. The trainee will inevitably accept the prevailing theory emphasized by the training committee/organization. Indeed, it is quite likely that the trainee has been attracted in the first place to the training programme by its special emphases and ways of working in therapy or counselling. I think it would be very unusual for a trainee to propose herself to a training committee without some very serious thought about the organization she was proposing to join. The in-house supervisor in such a situation inevitably carries a deeply felt responsibility for carrying the culture and theoretical emphasis of the organization in her work with the trainees.

The present schools of psychoanalysis are the most obvious examples of this suggestion. They are for the most part rivalrous and protective of their analytic exclusiveness. Some of them appear to exist in a condition of siege. In such circumstances the supervisor of trainees carries the message and ensures continuity, or 'purity', of the ideology.

The more recently formed organizations responsible for training the broader range of psychotherapists encompassing psychoanalytic therapy, gestalt therapy, the therapy of psychosynthesis, hypnotherapy, psychodrama, integrative therapy, cognitive analytic therapy, spiritual psychotherapy, family therapy, child therapy and so on have accompanying training schemes that are accredited by the UKCP. All these schemes will have elements of supervision built into their training programmes. Some of them are even now beginning to advance training programmes for supervisors, which are justified as being the natural extension of the role of the supervisor as a key person in the training of psychotherapists and counselling. At a later stage of this book I shall discuss the desirability or otherwise of such training programmes, examining some of the assumptions that appear to be built into the training programmes currently being advanced.

The world of counselling occupies a rather different history and cultural structure. Apart from the BACP, which is a general accrediting body, there are no training institutes in the sense of what we have understood as existing for psychotherapy training. Counselling training was taken up with enthusiasm by the world of further education. Indeed, in its earliest days there was a proliferation of quite low-level counselling courses on offer from colleges of further education sometimes based on the slimmest of professional resources. My own experience in a northern town was that a number of my clinical clients were 'training' in a local further education college counselling training group. These groups were virtually open-entry groups and sometimes proved attractive to people with emotional problems who were reluctant to identify their need for psychotherapy and found it more comfortable to enter counsellor training as a substitute for personal therapy. This is not intended to be a slight upon the people who go down this route to self-exploration and therapy. Indeed, the same might be said for many people in psychotherapy training. It would be interesting to find figures that would show how many trainee psychotherapists go on to become active psychotherapists after their initial training. It has been said on a number of occasions that the good therapist is the most experienced patient.

However, this background has been a persistent influence in the training of counsellors, and today, as I write, I am aware that there is a good number of universities that either directly promote or accredit professional counselling and supervision courses. The result has been to create a hierarchy of trainers and supervisors, many of them with advanced university qualifications. Every year there is an output of MA dissertations, and some students proceed to PhD level. At the sub-degree level there are a number of diploma courses available that act as an introduction to full training and qualification in supervision, where there will be accompanying supervised practical experience with clients. Thus there is a developing field for supervisors. Holloway (1995) notes that in the USA this area is highly developed and with it has come a plethora of publications concerning the training and qualification of counsellor supervisors working with counsellor trainees.

This phenomenon is now approaching the UK, and with it an emphasis upon an 'educational' approach to the practice of supervision. The educational context emphasizes learning and teaching, and the supervisory relationship takes on that colour in texts now being published (*Clinical Supervision* Holloway, 1995, *Supervising Counsellors and Therapists* Stoltenberg and Delworth, 1987 and *Training Counselling Supervisors* Holloway and Carroll, 1999). These books propose a model and sometimes a systematic approach to training supervisors, where learning experiences are systematized in layers of theory and activity. These can be learned and applied by supervisors and evaluated according to satisfactory or unsatisfactory exchanges in the supervisor/supervisee relationship (Inskipp and Proctor, 1995). The assumptions are didactic and cognitive and there is little room in many of the texts for any subjective evaluation of the emotional material that is being addressed, especially in terms of the emotional experience of the counsellor and the supervisor. This factor will be addressed in the next chapter, when I shall expand upon the notion of the relational approach to supervision in counselling and psychotherapy.

I have a further word of caution. It seems to me that, as more universities enter the counselling training field, the emerging subject of counselling psychology will become the dominant academic influence and the awards that go with it up to PhD level might come to be seen as the necessary prerequisites for the role of supervisor. This would certainly fit the prevailing university culture. If such a development takes place, the consequences are difficult to predict. I am not sanguine at the prospect.

# Chapter 3
# The relational approach

In this chapter I shall examine and discuss the nature of the relationship between the supervisor and the supervisee in the mutual learning process. I shall advocate what is called the relational approach.

The institutional approaches to training described in the previous chapter are a long way from the relational approach. The relational approach, adopted in psychotherapy supervision, is where the emphasis is upon a more equal exchange between trainee and supervisor: the exchange of mutual learning. The therapeutic and supervisory relationships of therapy are scrutinized with a special emphasis upon the subjective feelings experienced in both settings. This approach to supervision is the one that I advocate and practise with my supervisees. The subjective reactions of the supervisee are treated seriously as valuable material in the supervision process. At the same time the supervisee is encouraged to debate with the supervisor in a spirit of professional equanimity. This does not mean there is no room for discussion of theoretical ideas or the *actual* behaviour of the presented client in counselling or therapy. But there is no assumption that the trainee comes to supervision bereft of all knowledge relevant to her role as a counsellor or therapist. Quite the contrary.

The relational approach makes exactly the opposite assumption. It assumes that the counsellor/therapist is already in possession of valuable attributes towards the task of working as a counsellor or therapist. The trainee, being an adult human being, has already accumulated a rich harvest of personal and professional psychological and social experience. The trainee comes to the process of training with valuable assets that may be used to great advantage, once identified and activated. The therapist/counsellor is usually experiencing personal therapy and counselling. This is the very basis of so-called 'training analysis/therapy/counselling'. So the notion of the empty blackboard that has to be filled in the process of learning is rejected. Replacing it is the suggestion of a deeply personal store of knowledge and learning, existing in the trainee, that needs to be explored, to develop and expand the work of the trainee in preparing to become a counsellor or therapist. It should be acknowledged here that Carl Rogers was an early advocate of this view of learning. It is a matter of concern that his authoritative position is sometimes not always respected in contemporary trainee supervision practice

Accepting such an assumption puts the supervisor in a position of collaboration with the trainee where she calls upon the trainee to explore and marshal their existing and developing resources of learning towards working with the client or clients. In this respect the supervisor/supervisee relationship takes on a creative dynamic with great potential for the good practice of counselling and psychotherapy. The supervisor enters willingly into the uncertain space of feeling that the supervisee experiences with her client. The supervisor embraces the confusion and sometimes the fear of the supervisee as part of the supervision relationship. She does not attempt to produce pat or reassuring answers but rather works with the supervisee to understand and come to terms with the feelings that are being expressed. Sometimes these feelings result in bewilderment and confusion.

Mitchell (1988) proposes a similar paradigm within the therapeutic relationship where he insists upon the relationship between the client and her complex network of human of relationships, including the therapist, as the determining feature in human psychological life. He states this not to destroy the psychoanalytic view of the importance of the inner psychological life of the client, including her unconscious life, but rather to broaden and extend the therapeutic experience to utilize the psychoanalytic understanding within a new energetic context. My description of the relationship in the supervision room aligns itself alongside this position, which is why I call it the relational approach. Like Mitchell (1988), I do not think that supervisors should be afraid to enter the tangled world of transference and countertransference that the therapist/counsellor experiences. On the contrary, my view is that, if good work is to be done in supervision, entry to the emotional world of the supervisee is required and is nothing to fear.

**Example**

*Mary was a member of a creative therapy supervision group. She was training in psychodrama with a powerful psychodramatist, who both excited and encouraged Mary but at the same time could promote feelings of anxiety and failure in her when she found herself stumbling in the training process.*

*The supervisor was presented with these feelings in a very powerful way as Mary approached the end of her training. The trainer seemed reluctant to conclude the training and thus qualify Mary as a competent psychodrama psychotherapist. The situation was complicated by the fact*

*that Mary was already holding a social services post where she would have been expected to utilize her therapy skills. The supervisor had to be quite unafraid of entering Mary's world of confusion and distress. It would have been inappropriate to have distanced herself from the situation and sheltered behind a position of detachment and no comment.*

*Eventually, Mary sought the assistance of another group of psychodrama trainers to safely and successfully complete her training.*

In this instance the psychoanalytic/creative therapist, who was Mary's supervisor, had to follow the relational approach in her work with Mary. But this was not easily accomplished. The supervisor had to draw very close to Mary's feelings about her first trainers, especially the male in the training structure. The supervisor had to constantly monitor her own feelings about these trainers and how far she, too, could be drawn into feelings of anxiety and anger concerning their apparent treatment of their trainee. To have rejected this experience and retreated into a position of analytic 'interpretation' entirely limited to issues of transference would have left the trainee struggling with feelings of guilt and persecution.

Counsellors will find this suggestion easier to accept than traditional psychoanalytic therapists, but they should not make the mistake of believing that Mitchell (1995) was abandoning the belief that Freud's theories of the unconscious, early origins of pathology, defence mechanisms and psychic structure were of great significance. On the contrary, he insists upon the primacy of such ideas, while at the same time inviting contemporary psychotherapists to modify their approach to their clients (this, in my view, would include their supervisees) in order to get closer to their world of psychic disturbance and change.

This model is not a rejection of the educational aspect of the supervisor/supervisee relationship. Rather, it is simply a different approach aimed towards a common end.

It is worth noting at this point an emphasis made by Petruska Clarkson (1995, p. 293) where she observes, accurately in my opinion:

> Practitioners in the helping professions tend to be conscientious, well motivated and often hyper-critical of themselves. Concerns about 'doing damage', saying or doing 'the wrong thing' and appearing in an unfavourable light to colleagues, trainers, supervisors or peers seems to be on the increase.

I think this reflection simply emphasizes the need for an approach in which the emphasis is upon working together towards a good, creative end, rather than on a 'right' and 'wrong' approach, where issues of blame and inadequacy inevitably arise in the mind of the supervisee. Clarkson is clearly acknowledging the emotional context of supervision, where the trainee can easily begin to feel inadequate and guilty in the process of supervision, which is inevitable as the process opens up areas of doubt and uncertainty. The relational approach undermines the tension associated with this process. It substitutes a supervision relationship which is far less imbued with judgement of praise and blame. Its principal focus is one of enquiry.

Interestingly enough, Elizabeth Holloway (1995, p.7) draws attention to the importance of the supervisor/supervisee relationship in its emotional aspects, and this within a text that is, over all, highly didactic in its pronouncements.

She writes, discussing the empowerment of the supervisee:

> ... it is a sense of autonomy that comes from feeling capable of making a difference in one's world of skills that contributes to helping oneself and the world of others ... *Supervisors* [my emphasis] are well advised to allow the supervisees unique improvisation, adaptation and creation of methods and approaches. A supervisee cannot be expected to adhere to the supervisor's way of doing practice ...[a] challenging task for supervisors ... because they must confront their own narcissistic needs and issues of self-aggrandisement ...

Elizabeth Holloway is getting very close to my description of the relational approach in this statement. The trainee in a training organization will not lose out from such a view of learning in supervision. The organization need not worry that its dearly held precepts will be undermined in such a philosophy of learning. On the contrary, it is likely that the organization and its ideology will be enhanced by the sense of freedom and maturity such a stance encourages. Unfortunately, as a supervisor, as one who came from a progressive background of teaching trainee teachers and community workers, I have all too often listened to the complaints of trainees in psychotherapy and counselling as they suffer narrow didactic teaching methods where the information goes in one ear and out the other. The trainees are treated as passive recipients of knowledge, of which they have no previous experience, and little respect is accorded to their position as educated adults with a history of personal, social and psychological development. In other words, active, critical co-operation is not welcomed in the training situation when it is thus described.

### Example

*Sheila came to me for personal therapy as part of her training to become a psychoanalytical psychotherapist. She had recently retired early from a senior post in a well-established and distinguished university, where she had held senior departmental, teaching and research responsibilities; she was well equipped with learning theory. Her special subject was developmental psychology in which she was a recognized authority and author.*

*Throughout her training as a therapist I cannot recall her ever discussing any progressive or respectful approach by her teachers towards her university experience. On the contrary, she occasionally remarked somewhat ruefully upon the absence of interest shown by her teachers towards her previous professional experience. She noted the ignorance shown by her teachers of contemporary learning theory. In their exposition of psychoanalytical theory they appeared to be 'chalk and talk' teachers, maintaining the students in a passive, non-participative position.*

This mirrored my own experience some twenty years ago when I took early retirement from a senior academic teaching position, where I was the course leader for two degrees, both of which had large elements of developmental psychology as components of learning, and went to work sessionally in an NHS psychotherapy service. I had no wish to capitalize on my previous experience for the sake of status, but it always surprised me how utterly indifferent my psychiatric and psychotherapy colleagues were to my former life as a teacher in higher education, mainly working in the education of professional group workers and teachers. As for the medical staff of the hospital, I noted the attitude of the junior doctors when I was given a simple instructional role in their training as psychiatrists. What they wanted was notes they could write down together with model answers. I obliged. The medical model of learning was too entrenched for me to shift from my relatively humble position as a lay psychotherapist.

It is this cautious, conservative position of learning, which the trainee may well encounter within her training organization, that I feel must not be reinforced by her supervisor but, on the contrary, should be challenged in a creative, explorative discourse. While being respectful of the received culture of the institute/college or training organization, the supervision dialogue must show itself able to challenge it in a positive, developmental manner. This, to my mind, is the basis of the relational approach to supervision. For a supervisor to take up this position it is vital that the culture of supervision emphasizes independence and autonomy in the task of supervision. The supervisee must be encouraged to move towards an adult, competent position as a counsellor or therapist, where she is capable of handling the therapeutic relationship with a demanding client with confidence and capability, albeit with an awareness of her personal limitations as a therapist – a person who is not afraid to ask for help. To achieve this the supervisee needs to discover confidence in herself in understanding and working in a human relationship. In this respect I find myself entirely in agreement with Elizabeth Holloway (1995), quoted above.

The supervisor must be more than a mere transmitter of the values, techniques and the theoretical stances of the main training figures within the training organization. From this it can be deduced that the first loyalty of the supervisor is towards *her supervisee in the relationship with the presented client or group of clients*. In this sense it may be compared with the ethics of counselling and psychotherapy, where the first loyalty is towards the client in the therapeutic relationship. This does not mean that there are no other loyalties. Indeed, there are a number of instances where loyalties of a secondary order may come into play.

My description of relational supervision takes me back to Pedder (1986) again when he writes about supervision being more than an educational, but less than a therapeutic, relationship. There is a tension between the two, and my belief is that this tension can be the energetic, creative space in which supervision can best be conducted to the advantage of supervisee and supervisor alike. This is the relational position. If this is to be achieved, we need to take note of the findings described by Elizabeth Holloway (1995, p. 45) where she describes the power balance between supervisor and supervisee as being weighted towards the supervisor with consequences that will be felt in the relationship between them. Stoltenberg and Delworth (1987, pp. 168-169) emphasize this issue when discussing supervision that is drawn closely into the assessment procedures of training bodies. They draw attention to supervisor bias and special interest, which, when placed into the context of assessment of the trainee, can seriously distort the fairness of the assessment procedure. They write: '... the supervisory relationship is one of inherently unequal status, power and expertise.'

They advocate the supervisee's right to have choice in the matter of supervisor (p. 172) and outline the need for respect to be given to the role of supervisee in the supervision relationship.

My own view is that where it is known, or suspected, that the relationship is defective and experienced in persecutory or authoritarian terms by the trainees, there will be a serious distortion of the relationship between and supervisor and supervisee, which will make the creative, secure dialogue that I have described almost impossible. The relational approach is an attempt to redress the balance of power so that it sits more evenly between supervisee and supervisor, while remaining absolutely aware of its presence.

So far, this chapter has been concerned with the special experience of training. Now I want to give some space to the problem of the supervision of therapists and counsellors who are employed in institutional settings. These settings, in my experience, have either been doctors' practices, hospital psychotherapy or psychology services, educational organizations, including student counselling services, and large commercial and industrial organizations. Somewhat to my surprise, I have had a small but steady population of therapists and counsellors coming for supervision who are supported by their employers. Now this is to be applauded. It is rewarding for me in both financial terms and that of widening experience. It is of benefit to the counsellor or therapist concerned. It demonstrates that the employer respects and understands the place of supervision in the work of the counsellor/therapist and, finally, it is of benefit to the client. The *separateness* of the supervisor in this situation means that she can enjoy a great advantage in the supervision process. On the other hand, it does mean that the supervisor is placed in a position where there has to be intense alertness to work practices and cultures, which may be far away from the personal experience of the supervisor. This can hardly be stressed enough. The following experience is somewhat unusual, but illustrates the need for a flexible and accommodating attitude by counsellor and supervisor alike.

## Example

*John, an experienced and intelligent counsellor who had been bringing his clients to me for supervision for some years, came one day with a new and unique instance of his private practice to which I had to make a swift and understanding adjustment. He had taken on a consulting relationship with a small engineering firm that employed about thirty workers. Most of them were skilled working-class men and women; a few were related in one way or another to the proprietor of this private firm. The firm was active, busy and relatively prosperous. The 'boss' had, at sometime in his life, experienced mental and emotional distress, and felt he had benefited from psychotherapy, and he had decided to give support to his employees in a similar way if called upon to do so. The atmosphere was parochial and on the whole was experienced as beneficial by the employees. My supervisee was drawn into the network in what appeared to be a 'mothering' position and had to handle the transference 'idealization' from the proprietor with some care and discrimination. This was the theme of much of the supervision.*

*Although I personally would have been reluctant to enter into such a contract, I felt it was not my job as supervisor to place a judgemental comment on the situation. Rather, I decided to work with the supervisee in making it as properly beneficial as he could for everyone concerned. There was not so much conflict of outlook between myself and the supervisee as to threaten the supervision relationship. Quite the contrary, I regarded the therapist as being one of the most sensitive and insightful supervisees I had ever worked with.*

Most of the time we do not encounter such a closed and complex system of therapy when supervising therapists and counsellors working for clients employed within an organization. However, organizations throw up all sorts of challenges to counsellors, therapists and supervisors, and these are of a widely varying character.

The growth of counselling and therapy in organizations has been of an ad hoc character and there has not been one strong, steadying influence at work in determining the nature and theoretical orientation of these services. The greater part had been reflected in the use of counsellors in a wide variety of settings. Fewer psychotherapists have been drawn into the field, largely because fewer have been available or attracted by the conditions provided for the work. Partly the history and theoretical background of most psychotherapists, whatever their particular orientation, has not promoted or supported the placement of therapists in any numbers inside the structure of organizations. With the coming of employee assistance programmes this is changing, and it is becoming more common for psychotherapists to accept referrals through and within these agencies.

Clearly, modern business and public employers are responding to the need to provide a higher degree of care for their employees than used to be the practice some years ago, and there is much discussion of 'stress' in the workplace. This development must, for the greater part, be welcomed, if with reservation. The word 'stress' tends to be used as a catch-all and often masks quite complex and demanding behaviour on the part of clients, which might require more sensitive, insightful and descriptive explanation. We should remember, however, that sometimes 'stress' can be useful!

It has to be recognized that many therapists, counsellors and supervisors working for and on behalf of employing bodies sometimes find themselves faced with quite basic contradictions between their own methods and theories of good practice and the culture of the workplace. Sue Copeland (in Lawton and Feltham, 2000) makes the telling point that economic pressures play their part in this complex interplay of influences. She writes:

> ...the market place demands that counsellors work in settings other than private practice. They [the counsellors] have the choice to work in organizational contexts and may do so for economic reasons, with or without the knowledge and skills needed, or the theoretical orientation that dovetails with the counselling being offered in that context.

She comments, too, on how numbers of supervisors will not work within such a situation in order to avoid conflicts that may prejudice their professional values. For supervisors who do embrace the organizational challenge and take aboard counsellors or therapists for supervision who work within these contexts, the challenge is to find a way of working that does not prejudice their professional codes and ethics and at the same time recognizes the special needs of the organization. The kind of issues that are likely to arise may be as follows:

Information: how far should a counsellor or therapist share confidential, privileged information with an employer of the client, and what role has the supervisor in determining such an agenda? Supervision contracts should be explicit in this respect, and it rests upon the designated supervisor not to create any areas of ambiguity regarding this issue.

Confidentiality: closely aligned with the issues of information. How far should a therapist or counsellor concede the employer having a 'right to know' about any information or behaviour concerning a client drawn from the organization, even when it is argued that it is to the benefit of the client that the information should be shared? As above, the supervisor needs to make it clear in what situation the confidentiality of the situation would be broken in favour of a third person.

Reports: in what circumstances should a supervisor agree to produce a report on the work of the supervisee that is going to be scrutinized by third persons?

Supervision: to what extent is the supervisor 'in the pay' of the employer of the therapist or counsellor coming for supervision with a duty to report to the employer on matters concerning the supervisee? Where does the supervisee's responsibility begin and end, and to whom and in what order is her loyalty ordered? The important issue here is to ensure that the 'employer' is made fully aware of the professional position and ethics of the supervisor before any contract is agreed. Sometimes it is better for the supervisee to undertake paying the supervisor directly and then, in retrospect, claiming back supervision fees from the employer. This provides a symbolic statement of the position of the supervisor to the supervisee within the supervision relationship.

The BACP (*BACP Code of Ethics and Practice for Supervisors of Counsellors*, 1996) sets out certain guidelines between supervisee/client, supervisor/supervisee and organization/client. It stresses the need to recognize the difference between the management role in providing support to the employee and the role of the counsellor.

This is all very well and needs to be said, but in the end it comes back to the individual supervisor to interpret her role in relation to the organizational context she is presented with. The following example demonstrates the tension that can arise for a supervisor when a supervisee is placed in a position of professional risk by the actions of an employer who is paying for supervision.

**Example**

(This example is first referred to in the Introduction to this book.)

*This situation arose with a creative therapist working for a large hospital and placed within a day-unit provision. The therapist had a psychodynamic orientation and a professional interest and training in creative therapy. The phone rang one morning in the day unit and a senior nursing officer told the therapist to go to ward X to cover for the absence of the usual charge nurse. The therapist, having no medical or psychiatric training, felt the order was inappropriate and refused to go to the ward and provide cover, arguing that the patients would still be at an unacceptable risk if she did so. In other words, she was saying, 'I am not competent to meet the needs of such a ward and this instruction is unreasonable.'*

The therapist brought the issue to supervision and presented it as a key issue. She was being threatened with disciplinary procedures. After some thought I came to the conclusion that I should give the therapist my full professional support in her decision. I noted that ethical issues, professional boundaries and clinical appropriateness concerns were all present. Her trade union and professional body both came to her assistance. I found this support, coming from the trade union, very helpful, as she took on responsibility for aspects of the situation that would have not been easily addressed in supervision.

Nevertheless, the hospital went ahead with a disciplinary meeting where no decision was taken against the therapist, but neither was there any admission that the nursing officer concerned had behaved inappropriately. I found this last conclusion unacceptable, but I was not in a position to challenge it.

In fairness to the hospital management I am pleased to report that, although I had made a statement in support of the therapist concerned, they never wavered in paying my professional supervision fee, and they made no attempt to contact me to influence me in my judgement of the situation.

An interesting point arose associated with this case. Although virtually all accredited counsellors and psychotherapists belong to some kind of professional body, I think it unlikely that many of them belong to a trade union. In the case quoted above the influence and support of the professional officers of the trade union concerned, UNISON, proved invaluable and relieved the therapist of much of the day-to-day strain of dealing with the hospital management. Apart from providing professional support in supervision sessions I also set out the position of the therapist and her professional responsibilities in written evidence to be used at the discretion of the therapist and her advisers. Of course, many therapists and counsellors working within organizations will be in trade unions. But I am sure that those simply offering sessional support as counsellors, therapists or supervisors will not enjoy such protection. They would be well advised to seek it. I am a life member of NATHFE, which arose from my previous life as a lecturer in higher education, and I am grateful for its presence in my professional life.

Discussing this with a psychotherapist recently, who is employed by a large health authority, I was reassured when he told me that he was a member of a trade union (the MSF) operating within the hospital, and he thought an increasing number of therapists in NHS practice were following his example.

Before concluding this discussion of the issues that arise in organizational structures I feel it must be borne in mind that there can be no formulaic response that will anticipate the impact of organizational culture on the supervisory relationship. All that can be said is that supervisors need to be ready for this occurrence in an informed, non-defensive way, which will allow them to respond in a creative and authoritative way when they are faced with the challenge. It should be remembered that a professional body investigating a complaint against a member is obliged to be even-handed between the member of the public complaining and the member concerned. It will not specifically set out to defend the counsellor or therapist concerned. If the member needs an advocate in her defence, she has to provide it for herself, usually in the form of a lawyer. That may be satisfactory; it will be expensive. A professional indemnity insurer or trade union will carry out this task as part of its service to its membership.

As the satirist Tom Lehrer wrote, in a parody of the Scouts' motto: 'Be prepared, as through life you go along, don't be worried, don't be flustered, don't be scared ... be prepared!'

Before concluding this topic I would like to draw attention to the problem for counsellors and psychotherapists who work within a religious or spiritual perspective and look for 'healing' in the therapeutic relationship. They may experience great difficulty in finding a supervisor who can work comfortably and supportively with them. I note that in all my years of practice I have not met with a request to supervise a therapist working within a religious/ spiritual dimension. This may well be because I am probably known as a neo-Freudian psychotherapist.

My view is that if the supervisor, approached with such a request, cannot honestly support the nature of the counselling/therapy, she should, sensitively and politely, decline the responsibility. William West (1999) draws attention to some spiritually orientated therapists in supervision, revealing that they could not reveal certain spiritual experiences to their supervisor, because they felt such revelations would not be welcome and would produce discord.

My view is that such powerful belief positions, if not shared by the supervisor, will inevitably produce tensions that cannot be resolved in the usual provision of supervision. Unrevealed value positions in supervision is the antithesis of the relational approach in supervision and should be recognized as such.

In concluding this chapter I wish to stress again that I am not advocating any formulaic model for supervision. On the contrary, I believe a relational approach allows for great individual expression and supports a creative explorative way of being in the relationship both for the supervisee and the supervisor.

# Chapter 4
# Supervising private practice

In this chapter I shall be taking a close look at the relationship of supervisor to supervisee(s) within a private practice, noting the special characteristics that make for a climate of good, creative work and those that may impede or undermine the process. I shall be using some case examples to illustrate particular problems and experiences that best demonstrate the discussion.

Janice Scott (2000) writes:

> I take with me the unwavering support of my supervisor. When I walk into the therapy room she is with me. Her generosity and level of availability enables me to always remember that I am not alone with the horrors that can emerge with the client.

I believe that Janice Scott in her words 'level of availability' is actually describing an experience close to what I am calling the relational approach described in the previous chapter. But more about this later in this chapter.

As things stand at the moment, most supervisors come to their practice from a long-established position as valued therapists and counsellors. They may too have training responsibilities and, running alongside this, an established private practice of counselling or psychotherapy. Virtually all of them, in my experience, have been 'in supervision' as part of their professional lives as therapists and counsellors. Certainly this was true for me. I was accustomed to being a supervisee. I was involved for many years in the training field, working with both counsellors and therapists from a number of different disciplines. It was quite a natural progression to move into the area of supervision. The first request I had in my private practice was from three creative therapists asking me to set up a supervision group. I had experience as a supervisor in the NHS, but this was to be the first in private practice. I am grateful to those creative therapists now, in retrospect. Their initiative taught me a great deal. I approached the project as a learning experience and felt I was an equal among equals in working with these creative and capable therapists.

Two of these therapists were dramatherapists in practice and the other one was a dramatherapist in training as a psychodramatist. At that time I was both qualified and registered as a dramatherapist and psychodramatist with the appropriate professional bodies.

It is customary for creative therapists to enter supervision after qualification with a supervisor of their own choice. My relationship with them was based upon my years of practice as a dramatherapist and psychodramatist and my personal reputation as a therapist and supervisor. I was not then, or now, trained as a supervisor. I shall be discussing the particular requirements of the supervisor working with creative psychotherapists, in more detail, at a later stage of this book.

There is, now, a developing movement towards providing training for supervisors. I shall say more about this but for the moment would simply observe that the issue for me is not whether supervisors could benefit from training, but rather what *kind* of training is most appropriate for their needs. And who should provide it?

Like most psychotherapists and counsellors I had, of course, received supervision at different times and from different people. On the whole it had been a good experience, although I had one supervisor who was somewhat punitive towards me, and, I would stress, to others in his care. I would have probably welcomed training as a supervisor at this point in my life but none was available where I lived and worked. Had I gone to such a training course I know what I would have looked for. I would have wanted an extended and in-depth examination of the relationship with the supervisor and found a way of getting a better understanding of how and what we discussed and how we communicated with one another. I would have valued an experiential form of learning. In the event, in becoming a supervisor, I had received no such training, and all I could do was to turn to my experience of being a supervisee in training, and a therapist in supervision. From the very beginning I sensed that the first principle of supervision was to support the therapist and, through her, the client we were working with. Of course it is, in the event, much more complicated than that simple statement suggests. Hence this book!

Another very early experience was the supervision of a counsellor with a demanding private practice. One of the most important features of this relationship was that it was desired and sought after by the counsellor and, very importantly, paid for on the basis of a monthly fee and a session lasting one and a half hours.

Early on in our opening discussion we settled the frequency and length of the supervision sessions and timings. The discussion felt familiar. It had the tone of a private psychotherapy contract. Implicitly we were recognizing together the importance of boundaries, and they came up as imperatives at the very outset of our conversation. For the counsellor, working in private practice, there was nothing unusual about any of this. He recognized the format I was proposing, and it all felt like familiar territory. It was a comfortable discussion. I even recall offering a cup of coffee, a friendly gesture that was accepted with a grin. He, too, was aware of a shift away from the formality of the clinical session towards something that was closer but not the same. I soon discovered that the supervision was not only to be focussed upon the clinical work with a particular client but also included what I shall describe as the counsellor's 'whole practice'.

As the counsellor left at the end of the session I remember reflecting with pleasure on the visit, noticing in myself a degree of satisfaction, at an emotional level, which I was not accustomed to experience with my clinical clients. Freud warned psychoanalysts to remember they were working at a 'deficit' with their patients. Their own need for gratification had to be repressed in favour of the patient. I have frequently thought of his remarks when I have noticed a feeling of fatigue and disinterest arising in me if I have seen 'too many' patients in a particular day.

For people coming to work from another profession where a high degree of satisfaction in the workplace was an open and recognized feature of their lives, moving into counselling and therapy was difficult and different. For many therapists even the presence of 'chitchat and pleasant gossip' with their colleagues is very restricted when working in specialist psychotherapy units. For private practitioners working alone, it is almost always entirely absent.

The experience of supervision is different. The tone and colour of the work is different, especially when the work is with a colleague, as supervisee, who is at an equally competent level of work. This colleague is usually at the same level of training and practice as the supervisor. Reservations concerning status and power, expressed by Stoltenberg and Delworth (1987), do not enter the framework with such force. The gratification I felt was the natural product of the exchange between myself and the counsellor. We got on well together, 'spoke the same language', although we were from differing training backgrounds. The cup of coffee had said something about being together. We were relaxed with one another. On the other hand, the therapist side of me was aware that, in this relationship, transference would undoubtedly occur. It was up to me as the supervisor to recognize it when it occurred and find a way of working with it. My own view on transference is the same as Yalom's (1975, pp. 191-220): that it is a natural phenomenon; it occurs in all our relationships, personal and professional, and occupies a special place in psychotherapy and counselling, which needs acknowledgement. All counsellors and therapists will have encountered it in their training and know intimately the force of its presence.

Out of this meeting came a long and fruitful period of supervision experience from which we both benefited. I noted, too, the strong contrast with my clinical sessions. It could be said that as therapists and counsellors we may get deferred gratification, whereas with supervision the gratification is more immediate and present.

The first requirement is to respond to the desire of the counsellor wanting supervision, who is identifying the therapist as fulfilling this role, and to understand the significance of the choice and proposal. The impact of choice should not be underestimated. Shortly before beginning to write this book I had two senior psychotherapists approach me for supervision. There came a glow of self-satisfaction, a sense of reassurance; it was quite primitive. I had been chosen (recognized as fit) to work with two people who I knew enjoyed status and respect as psychotherapists and who occupied senior positions. More recently I have been approached to supervise a team of psychodramatists, working together in a community setting, for supervision. Again, I was very pleased to be approached.

The second requirement is for the supervisor to arrange a secure meeting in which a discussion can take place about the needs of the counsellor and the suitability of the therapist for this task. It also needs to be recognized that many of us come from different training backgrounds, and we have internalized a set of values, ideas and procedures that have to be understood, acknowledged and mutually assessed. We may meet a potential supervisee and know, quite quickly, that it would be almost impossible to offer supervision, working from our own knowledge base and the deeply subjective feelings that arise in us. If this happens, it should be quite quickly understood and acted upon. The job of the supervisor, then, is to help the counsellor or psychotherapist find another potential supervisor.

On the other hand, the instance I have described above is that of a person-centred counsellor seeking supervision with me, knowing that I occupy a psychoanalytic position as a therapist. However, the sophistication of his own post-training experience drew us quite close to each other theoretically. He also knew that I had a deep respect for the work of Carl Rogers (1967).

My third injunction at this point is to establish a therapeutic contract. This means addressing such issues as frequency of meeting, times and length of meeting, boundaries of time and place, confidentiality, communications, fees and an understanding concerning the scope of the supervision being offered. By this it is meant that parts of the supervisee's work may well be quite appropriate for the supervision that is being offered, other parts not. This cannot be known in advance; it is a matter for negotiation. The supervisor may offer other kinds of support. For example, the supervisor may well agree that the supervisee can ask for a reference from the supervisor when trying to gain employment. This, again, is a matter for negotiation. The question of telephone contact can be discussed. The question of fee needs to be addressed and agreement reached concerning notice of cancelled or postponed sessions. None of these issues should be unfamiliar to an experienced counsellor or therapist; they are quite close to the usual procedure when setting up a contract with a client for therapy or counselling.

The next issue to address is the assumption that the supervisee may be a colleague, with whom there may be social and professional contact outside the supervision room. If this is the case, it is probably necessary to explicitly acknowledge the nature of the situation, agreeing that the supervision contract applies in the space for supervision, and the outside contact will not be violated in any way by inappropriate material that belongs in the supervision relationship. Here a 'dual relationship' (Clarkson, 1997) is acknowledged and described in the contract that protects both the supervisee and supervisor concerned.

Thought needs to be given to the scope of supervision. Although it is likely and probable that the supervisee will want supervision in respect of named clients from her practice, it should also be understood that other areas of employment that the supervisee enjoys may need the attention of the supervision relationship.

Ye Min makes a telling point in this respect in his contribution to Reflections at the end of this book. I have coined the phrase 'whole practice' to cover this eventuality. The term 'whole practice' may be limited to the private day-to-day work with individual clients, seen in an entirely private context. Sometimes the supervisee will have other contracted private work, which needs supervision, and assistance is required in looking at the shape, direction and practice of her whole employment as a counsellor or therapist. An obvious example would be employment in a GP practice, which would almost certainly be part time. The supervisor is usually seen as the best person to support such a broad evaluation of the character and impact of the therapeutic work upon the therapist. Counsellors and therapists sometimes work in a broad spectrum of employment situations, and this needs acknowledgement.

It should be remembered that Ye Min is working in an educational context and the supervisor would have to acknowledge the cultural shift involved for the therapist accustomed to a therapeutic milieu.

Obviously, occasionally, the material of the supervision relationship gets close to that of therapist and client. If the supervisee has an ongoing therapeutic relationship elsewhere, the supervisor is enabled to refer this to the supervisee and to suggest where the material is best presented. It is more difficult when that situation does not exist. The most important action is to acknowledge the character of the material coming to the supervision experience and question how appropriate it is to the situation. The experience must be resolved to the satisfaction of the supervisee and supervisor alike. It needs to be remembered that the supervision/supervisee relationship is embedded in a dialogue. This dialogue can be described as a subjective voice speaking and listening to another subjective voice, which in turn listens. Each reflects upon the voice of the other. I think this to be true of the counselling relationship as well as the psychoanalytic relationship. In each a high degree of subjective attention is paid to the other; we listen intensely.

To be fair to Freud, it should be acknowledged that this is perhaps the greatest debt we owe to psychoanalysis: the need to listen with unswerving subjective attention to the voice of the other. To my mind this, too, is the central requirement of the supervision relationship. I have deliberately emphasized the word 'subjective' as against the word 'objective'. This is not to say there is no such thing as objectivity. The first word we give for a stone is the word 'stone'. That is its objective descriptive noun. The stone may go on to be called a missile, a weapon, a work of art or a tool; it may be invested with emotional, even moral, qualities and so on. Then we enter the world of subjectivity, a subjectivity arising from the idea of use and symbol. Relationships may strive for a degree of objectivity, but the reality is that the greater part of any relationship is its subjectivity, based on the way it is implemented and experienced. The stone remains, in the first instance, a stone. I am reminded of a wonderful television documentary on the life of Wittgenstein, where he was depicted walking through an orchard striking each tree he encountered with a stick, saying out loud:

> '*This* is a tree and *this* is a tree and *this* is a tree.'
> And so on!

At a later point in this book I shall be looking more closely at ethical issues, but within the context of this chapter there are some relatively simple issues to be stated. The first and obvious one is that the contract should be honoured by the supervisor in its word and spirit. The relationship should also be respected and the boundaries kept; the supervisee must not be exploited in any way, and, if either party wishes to change the relationship, it should be openly acknowledged and agreed upon. The obvious area is that of the sexual relations where either, or both of the parties, become attracted to each other. More subtly, the issue of friendship may become a problem. If the supervisor and supervisee become too friendly, the process of supervision may suffer. This is not a matter of definitives. I cannot state how warm a friendship may be allowed to become, or at what point it may prove an impediment to the work in hand. But the possibility needs to be recognized and discussed.

**Example**

*I had a very clever and able man in supervision with me for some years. During these years a number of personal crises occurred in this man's life. He was in therapy and, although I 'knew' about them in a relatively superficial way, he took most of these experiences into his personal therapy. I do know my unshakeable support for him in his work impacted upon his feelings for me and mine towards him. I found him a most rewarding client. We shared cultural interests especially in literature and general cultural and professional affairs. I suspect we read the same newspaper! Sometimes I noticed we spent a good ten minutes simply warming up to each other before starting on the work in hand. One day he walked in and announced he wanted to leave the relationship with me and seek new supervision. I was rather shocked. There had been no lead up to this decision. However I discussed the announcement with him without any real difficulty and we eventually parted on good terms. This occupied my thoughts for some time, and, on reflection, I came to the conclusion that in some way or another our relationship had changed from being professional to become more like a friendship. It had got out of balance. For this development I felt I had to take the main responsibly, not he.*

Just as in the present psychotherapeutic and counselling climate what is described as 'dual relations' (Clarkson, 1997) is heavily frowned upon and excites condemnation from most practitioners, so we have to recognize that such criticism can be taken too far. The social relationship between the supervisor and supervisee, based upon genuine social standing and commitment, probably of some duration, should not be bracketed with that of the therapist and the client in therapy.

Clarkson (1997, p. 314) draws attention to the essential inequality of the relationship in the supervisor/supervisee connection and is gloomy about the outcome when that relationship becomes sexualized and even marriage occurs. She states: 'there are few, if any, which have stood the test of time ... the patient (supervisee) ended up not so much exploited as exploiting.'

While not wishing to enter into any dispute with Petruska Clarkson, indeed, I respect her views, I would simply state her personal experience is necessarily limited and she is quoting from personal observation.

Clarkson (1997, p. 318) also describes a social/professional situation; it occurs in conference hall where a number of dual relationships are observed:

I could identify my current analyst, my current supervisor, someone who was currently in supervision with me, the wife of a current client, the lover of a past client, the ex-wife of a colleague, my partner's ethics charge, I had sat on the complaints board during the case; the analyst of someone in supervision with me at the time, the friend of an old friend of mine who was at this time on the opposite side of the political fence.

Fleas on the back of fleas upon the back of fleas, and so on and so on! Most of us have experienced something like this from time to time. The world of counselling and psychotherapy is very small. I am reminded of attending the annual UKCP conference where all sorts of past relationships are encountered again in a new setting. Recently, I cried off attending a local seminar because I did not want to be meeting and discussing certain topics in a public way, within the presence of supervisees of the present and past. As I explained to a colleague: 'I know I would get too excited.'

Along with ethical issues associated with boundaries stands the problem of abuse (Kaberry 2000). It is difficult to know how frequently abuse in supervision is experienced. I had an experience with a senior psychotherapist, in supervision, where I felt neglected and unrespected. I would turn up at the agreed time for supervision only to be left kicking my heels in a public corridor for anything up to thirty or forty minutes before I was seen by the supervisor. This happened frequently. Strangely, I found it impossible to address my feelings with him, and I did not complain to other colleagues or friends. I wonder why? A transference issue I would guess. Kaberry (2000, pp. 44–45) writes:

> Many of the participants [in her study] felt frightened to reveal what had happened to them in case they were 'blamed' or 'psychopathologised' by other members of the profession. They were aware that other counsellors and supervisors would not want to believe their colleagues could perpetrate abuse.

I would add that some of them would not recognize the abuse as abuse, or simply interpret it in way that rendered it harmless. I think that was more the case as far as I was concerned. My supervisor was known to be distinguished and 'tough', even mildly eccentric. The irony was that, once we actually got going in the session, I rapidly forgot my resentment and found benefit from the work we did together.

The nature of abuse is not easily defined, but at the emotional level we usually know when we have experienced it! But we do not always act upon the knowledge. Masson's (1992) description of the manner in which he was treated by his analyst, in his training therapy in Canada, suggests that he was the victim of the most insensitive abusive behaviour. Interestingly enough, he does not himself identify it in that way to the point of leaving the relationship, he stuck with the analyst through thick and thin, even giving credit where he could. Stuart Sutherland (1976, pp. 16–25) reports what amounts to psychological abuse in the psychoanalytical situation, nearer to home, when he suffered a most distressing emotional breakdown. His book is a vivid personal account of the problem of getting sensitive, carefully understood treatment, when deep despair afflicts a human being. What is very important is having others confirm our painful experience. The more subtle examples of abuse can leave us confused. For example, the look of contempt from a supervisor when we get muddled in our assessment of a client, the impatient interruption that exposes us momentarily as stupid and ignorant or, as in my own case, the casual abuse of boundaries being ignored can affect us and distress us and leave us puzzled and uncertain concerning the validity of our experience (Kaberry, 2000).

In a later chapter I shall be dealing with issues of abuse more fully and in greater detail. In contrast the following sets out quite a different view and experience.

Pamela Ashurst (1993) writes:

> Supervision must have as its *raison d'être* the development of the supervisee so that he or she will become a more effective, confident and skilled psychotherapist. As in musical education, natural aptitude, motivation and personality will influence development and performance. Supervision can provide the framework for the development of both therapist and therapy but the therapist will be making a solo appearance; although the music of therapy will be created during each therapy session. If the supervisor intrudes too powerfully into the therapy, spontaneity and creative growth in the therapist will be stifled.

Although this piece refers specifically to the training of junior doctors in psychotherapy, much of it could be applied to counsellors and lay psychotherapists in training. The reference and comparison with making music is, I think, very appropriate.

Going back to the earlier statement that supervision is 'more than teaching but less than therapy' (Pedder, 1986), I would draw attention to what Szecsody (1990) describes as the 'mutative situation', where a favourable learning condition exists. He puts first and foremost the notion of the 'learning alliance', which immediately brings to mind the notion of the therapeutic alliance. It indicates a recognition of the 'mutuality of goals' as Szecsody (1990) describes it. He goes on to say that the complex quality of the relationship depends upon the 'personal qualities' of trainee and supervisor that the task of the supervisor, in attending to the work of the supervisee with a client, is to give due regard to:

> *how this actual patient with her unique personality expresses herself in her interaction with the Therapist and how this unique Therapist experiences this, reacts, interacts, thinks and feels about her (the client) and their interaction* [his emphasis].

This is the essence of the supervision relationship.

What is being described here is a relational approach to learning which combines therapeutic and educational values. The emphasis is upon the 'uniqueness' of the people concerned, within their roles as therapist and client; it indicates emphatically a value that goes beyond a system or model of supervision.

Ashurst (1993, p. 176.) suggests that Fordham (1982) contends that during supervision a supervisor should not evaluate or judge the student's capacities but facilitate the development of *what is available* (my emphasis). Although this sounds a simple statement, in reality it contains layers of complex meaning. After all 'what is available' is in itself unknown until the supervision is developed and explored. I believe it is this intimate and accepting position that is often sought when the therapist asks for private individual supervision.

My view is that the proposals of Holloway and Carroll (1999) which are currently emerging for training supervisors, with their emphasis upon structured task learning, need to take into account the values described by Szecsody. In my view it is essential that these human values do not get lost or obscured in the desire to produce coherency and effectiveness, in the training situation. In certain colleges the practice of modular learning and assessment, with stated, specific aims of knowledge and skills acquisition, are not, by themselves, very appropriate to the task of supervisor and supervisee alike.

This does not mean that there is no intellectual content or cognitive exchange. What it does mean is that the form and value of the supervision acts as a permanent guide and indicator to the supervisee and supervisor in their work together. The work can be brisk and demanding.

Currently I have a supervisee who does not hesitate to cry out, quite forcibly, 'No! It's not like that at all, not at all; you've got it wrong!' I believe the freedom to express disagreement so strongly and openly is a measure of the strength of our relationship with each other and is to be welcomed and valued. I have experienced working with newly trained and qualified therapists and counsellors who simply want from me at a certain moment in the supervision some information, which their lack of experience denies them. I do not hold back unless I detect another agenda in the request. Even then I continue the dialogue to enable us to examine the request at the two levels of intention. Simply because a question can overlay another concern does not mean that the original question is of no importance.

I have mentioned the newly trained and qualified therapist. I was slightly amazed and surprised to read the view of the late Nina Coltart (1993, p. 9) that:

> I ... make it clear that supervision comes to an end very shortly after qualification ... I consider that, unless the work is very shaky, the sooner the newly qualified therapist is out on his/her own, the better.

She is talking about trainees who have qualified as therapists to whom she has been the supervisor. She then goes on to advocate the importance of self-reliance. I couldn't agree more. But here I part company from her reasoning.

I do not believe that the relational approach to supervision undermines that desired self-reliance. On the contrary, I think, when well done, it will promote confidence in the supervisee and emphasize the growth towards self-reliance. If the relationship is right, it will challenge dependency or, even worse, sycophancy.

I would reject the concept that supervision simply increases dependency any more than good counselling or psychotherapy does. Of course, it could if it were badly done. It is possible that a supervisor exploiting a transference relationship of idealization, either wittingly or unwittingly, might easily build up an unhealthy relationship of dependency in the supervisee. But a sensitive and well-informed supervisor would be quick to spot the development of such a relationship, dealing with it in a proper professional manner, which would strengthen the supervisee's independence and undermine a tendency to dependency.

I stand with Clarkson (1995) when she writes:

> Supervision, which is an integral part of the primary psychotherapy training, ideally continues for the rest of the professional's practising life. It does not stop at a licence to practise independently but finds new and more challenging scope for growth, support and development.

In closing this chapter I think it sensible to state that, although I think the essence of effective supervision lies in the quality and character of the relationship between supervisor and supervisee, it is as well to remember that the basic conditions must be in place and maintained:

1. A good, pleasant, comfortable inviolable meeting place where both parties can feel secure and uninterrupted is provided. No telephones present, please – mobiles turned off!
2. A mutually agreed contract is in place where timing and frequency, fees and a statement of ethics and confidentiality and the conditions of supervision is in place.
3. A relationship that supports, challenges and informs: the relational approach.

It is worthwhile considering briefly the issue of references. The first time I was asked to be a referee for a supervisee in supervision with me I momentarily hesitated. I had not encountered the request before, and I wondered how to frame a response and what my position should be. I had always rejected the 'judgemental' position, and, indeed, I had never been pressed to do so in the circumstances where I worked. There was, too, the issue of money. Should I charge my supervisee for the time and trouble of composing a reference? This is a tricky one. Should it be possible to 'buy' a reference? I had known a senior counsellor, responsible for the supervision of a number of practising counsellors, who regularly charged a fee for writing references. I thought long and hard and decided I would not. I now tell supervisees that the supervision fee includes any writing that I may need to do on their behalf.

I eventually agreed to provide a reference to support the application of the supervisee, and my name went on to the appropriate form. I decided, in consultation with the supervisee, that the reference would be shown to the supervisee before I submitted it to the prospective employer. The employer would be informed of this by me.

I have followed this procedure ever since without any difficulty arising.

# Chapter 5
# What belongs where:
# the relationship between
# therapy and supervision

I have always believed that when thinking about therapy we need to hold two ideas in view at the same time. The first idea is that of reparation: putting something right that is wrong in life, to some degree or other. The second idea is that of good living: maintaining the rightness and goodness of the living experience.

In this chapter I shall be primarily describing what is implied by reparation, especially when it is pursued in a therapeutic relationship. Following this description, I shall relate the experience of therapy to supervision and contrast and compare the experience of both.

Reparation is quickly understood as a description of what many counsellors and therapists are doing for much of the time in their working lives. Many people seek the help of counsellors or psychotherapists because, at a certain point in their lives, they feel they need help. Circumstances vary, ranging from the most obvious precipitating causes, such as death of a loved one, to some other highly disturbing personal loss or trauma. There are less obvious, even mysterious, life experiences that give rise to anxiety, sadness or depression or the failure of important relationships. The counsellor or therapist enters the life of the client as a healing presence and initiates a relationship of acceptance and understanding that enables the client to consider the possibility of change.

The relationship is a complicated one. It promotes confidence and revelation, introspection, description and explanation. Depending on the orientation of the therapist, counsellor or psychologist, the relationship will develop a special kind of character, which is markedly different from what the client normally encounters in everyday life. The intimacy of the sexual relationship, family encounters or disclosures to 'best friends', important as they are, still differ in quality from the experience in the therapy space. I would argue that the therapeutic relationship is unique and special, in the sense of it not being commonly found in the usual social scene as far as most people are concerned. In part this difference is a product of the character of the material communicated between therapist and client, but another part is in the style and manner of the communication where the therapist acts for the most part in a spirit of the 'denial' of personal needs in her relationship with the client. The client usually recognizes this at an early stage and responds with understanding towards what might seem at first to be a neutral stance on the part of the therapist. Of course, the mirror-like qualities of the psychoanalytic therapist are very different from those of the person-centred counsellor, but, nevertheless, each from their own training and traditions pays respect to the fact that the client is there to be served in a spirit of non-exploitation towards therapeutic ends. The counsellor or therapist must look for personal gratification elsewhere.

Having said that, it must be remembered that each therapist and counsellor is a particular individual with a particular manner of being in the therapeutic situation. For example, the notion that the mirror position does not convey a meaning of the position of the therapist in response to the therapeutic dialogue is, in my view, nonsense. All of us, without exception, have a personality that communicates spontaneously, often unconsciously, with those around us. The signals we give are recognized by others, interpreted and responded towards. This happens everywhere, within the counselling and therapy situation and everywhere else.

**Example**

*A psychotherapy training group some years ago. Ten of us are sitting in the circle and the group psychotherapist watches us with a high degree of silent attention. We are very quiet today. The silence is maintained. Some of us, if not all, are covertly scrutinising the group therapist. He has said nothing since we came into the room. Will he break the silence? It is almost as if, in my perception, he is being put to the test. He sits, apparently comfortably in the situation, and then from his coat pocket he gets out a small tin of tobacco and some Rizla papers and begins to roll a cigarette. He does not speak. None of us comments. But we are all busily interpreting inside ourselves the meaning of this distracting act.*

Obviously, some readers would think that his behaviour was inappropriate. Therapists are not supposed to smoke in front of their clients. Some might imagine that his act was very exceptional. Well, it was certainly particular to him. But each of us has particularities. I knew a group analyst who spent much of his therapy time looking at the floor.

**Example**

*This scene occurs some years ago. I am attending a lecture and video presentation given by a leading psychoanalyst who works in an organiza-*

*tional setting. She is presenting a video of a one-to-one session with a patient, allegedly with the patient's permission. I am caught up in the excitement of the moment, watching visual and oral evidence of this distinguished therapist actually 'in action'. All of a sudden my attention wanders off the principal visual and oral signals from the video and I see in the corner of the screen a hand, the therapist's, move briefly into shot. She is picking up a coffee mug. The position of the camera, behind the therapist's head, does not show any more of the therapist, but I am shocked.*

In the discussion afterwards I keep my shock to myself until the discussion begins to touch on the subject of transference and I can hold back no longer. I reveal my feelings about the sight of the hand and the coffee mug. There is a silence. The therapist does not respond. I can feel the disapproval of the rest of the seminar group and the chairperson. I have revealed the fact that the 'emperor is not wearing any clothes'.

**Example**

*More recently I had cause to seek personal therapy again after a break of some years. I had never met the therapist before. Indeed, that is why, among other reasons, I had chosen her. At our first meeting she was very restrained and 'cool'. I had some difficulty in 'reading' her. The last thing I wanted was a cold, distant therapist who would not connect with me. Neither did I want a sympathetic, emotionally available, reflective therapist who would draw too closely into my space of emotional disturbance. I wanted a figure who could contain distress, recognize my autonomy and individuality as a human being and work with me towards an understanding of my inner and outer world. To find this in her I gave special attention to her non-verbal signals (Renton, 1981). I believe these to be the most subtle and unconscious activities that convey a wealth of meaning to the observer. After about three sessions I felt quite confident that I had received the unconscious assurances of what I wanted from my therapist, and I proceeded to work. Gradually she loosened up! And I did too.*

I offer these anecdotes not as evidence of substantial research but merely to illustrate my own experience of training, therapy and working as a psychoanalytical psychotherapist, where the proposition of distance and mirror-like stances has been advocated. Whilst respecting the purpose of such a position in the therapy room, I remain sceptical of its actuality. Our present-day understanding of all the conscious and unconscious signals we offer to clients, revealing many aspects of our personality and feelings, makes me question the absolute, or naïve, suggestion that we remain essentially unobserved as to our *actual* attitudes and beliefs. And everything the client 'picks up' can be attributed to transference. Holding an objective position, for example, is a useful concept but needs to be treated with caution when it leads to denial by the therapist that actual feelings towards the client exist and are active within her. I had a little theoretical quarrel recently with a leading group analyst who recommended the group therapist 'do nothing' in certain circumstances in the therapy room.

My view is very simple. There can be no possibility of 'doing nothing' in the therapeutic situation. The therapist is always doing something and so is the client or group members, whatever the case may be. Having approached the subject of the therapist's denial of self in the therapy room somewhat sceptically, I must also assert that the imperative still remains: that as therapists and counsellors we monitor ourselves carefully in the therapy situation, to restrain the greedy aspect that craves attention in all of us. So, while the 'mirror position' suggestion may be ultimately unobtainable, it remains a reasonable ideal to be worked towards.

I have been describing these experiences to illustrate the special conditions of psychotherapy and counselling. There are other less important conditions that are very specific to the practice of counselling and psychotherapy. It must be one of the rare activities where boundaries are maintained with such a degree of scrupulousness and where time, place and person (the traditional unities) are so sensitively observed (Feasey, 1999, p. 31). But these qualities are not exclusive to therapy; there are other professions and activities that pay a great deal of attention to this emphasis on structure. However, the concerns I have highlighted here so far need to be addressed when considering the relationship of therapy to supervision, and it is the latter that I now address.

As in psychotherapy and counselling it is the nature of the relationship that defines the character of supervision and places it in the professional spectrum of therapy. Although this relationship stands as special in its own category of a supervision relationship, it reflects itself in the psychotherapeutic relationship.

Indeed, Yalom (1975, p. 507) writes:

> the supervisory session is no less a microcosm than the therapy group and the supervisor would be able to obtain much information about the therapist's behaviour in his therapy group by attending to the behaviour in supervision. By implication it is being suggested that the supervision situation invites a therapeutic response by the supervisee.

Obviously, Yalom is referring to group psychotherapy.

Robertson (in Portman 1999, p. 96) in an interesting chapter on supervision in dramatherapy states: 'During supervision the therapy session is reproduced very closely to its original form, but at the same time takes on a life of its own.' I agree with her. She also goes on to discuss the therapeutic nature of the supervisor/supervisee relationship, concluding: 'In other words, a supervisory session with a professional is different from a therapy session with a client. The difference can be compared to a relationship between peers versus the relationship between parent and child.'

I find the description of the therapy relationship as being between 'parent and child' somewhat simplistic. I believe it has many representations, which may occur simultaneously in the therapy relationship. However, I do think her point is well enough put to emphasize the difference between supervision and therapy in a professional context.

Both for Yalom and Robertson the likelihood is that the context of supervision either is in the group or relates to therapeutic group work, but I am convinced the same reasoning applies to working with therapists in an individual situation.

Stoltenberg and Delworth (1987, pp. 168-9) observe: '... the supervisory relationship is one of inherently unequal status, power and expertise; and the relationship possesses *therapy-like* qualities,' (my emphasis).

The implication is that in the counselling and psychotherapy relationship the client is in the lesser position as far as the exercise of power is concerned, and this is reflected in the supervision relationship. It seems inevitable that the 'therapy-like' qualities, referred to by these authors, establish a framework of work where the supervisor, wittingly or unwittingly, exercises a high degree of control. This is a reflection of the position as outlined by Robertson, quoted above.

I think these assertions are undeniable and a feature of the supervisory relationship that needs to be acknowledged by anyone working in that role. At some times supervision comes very close to therapy. The closeness of the two roles, however, should not blind us to the differences between them; although I have to admit there have been a number of occasions when a client in supervision had presented me with material that could have been appropriately raised in the therapy situation, the emphasis is on *could have been*, not *should have been*.

## Example

*John had been working with me as a supervisee for a number of years. He was highly intelligent and very sensitive in his work with his clients. It was this aspect of my work that I enjoyed most with him as he demonstrated his ability to work empathetically with his clients while remaining well able to observe the process. I regarded him as my equal, although I imagine he had other thoughts about me! One day he came complaining of being completely stuck and stifled in his work with a young woman client, who defended herself with sustained, absolute silences of some duration. John confessed that when this happened he could not think; he became numb with a kind of stupid frustration. We discussed this feeling for some while, and he gradually began to let go of the young female client and reminisce about the past and his memories of long moments of threatening silence that would sometimes engulf his mother and father at the meal table, when he and his sisters would sit frozen with anxiety, waiting for a ferocious family row to burst out.*

The therapeutic issue for the supervisor is to know, or at least attempt to establish in the supervision conversation, at what level to approach this material. Where the client is 'in therapy' at the time of this kind of disclosure, in a sense the supervisor 's responsibility is made lighter. The client can be drawn to discuss the revealed material in her therapy, and this can be achieved in a caring and sensitive manner. However, where the therapist is not currently 'in therapy' another situation arises.

In the instance given I knew the therapist was not at that time seeing another therapist for personal therapy; so I worked with the material presented. Of course, as an experienced therapist, he knew quite well what the implications were of his own experience as a child, at the family meal table, and its repercussions in the therapy room with the client. We did not need to analyse or discover it. It was true, too, that the fact of his client being a young woman had played a substantial part in activating the memory. Her presence took him back to his sisters and their shared feelings of fear and tension as they waited for the explosion. We discussed the feelings he had of 'stupidity' and of being 'frozen' in relation to his client and her desire to protect herself by controlling the therapy session, through the medium of silence. As a child he had tried to remain safe by being silent. It had proved a useless defence. His client's silence was proving quite negative and unproductive, but he realized also that she had to discover this for herself. She was evidently trying to do so, and the evidence was in her unfailing and punctual attendance at the therapy sessions.

This example illustrates how close the supervision session sometimes gets to the therapy session. As supervisors, we are inevitably going to be offered material from time to time that *might well be worked with in a therapy session*. But I stress again this is not the imperative *should*.

Stoltenberg and Delworth (1987) quite properly raise the issue of authority and power and the inevitable feelings of inferiority, and even of domination, that might well be felt by the supervisee in the supervision session. This is a tricky matter. Most supervisors will reject the notion that they set out to dominate or control, in an unhealthy way, the work of the supervisee. But psychoanalytical psychotherapists will appreciate, from their training, that the power of the parental figure is very evident to them in both the psychotherapy session and the supervision session. Counsellors, trained to have a different framework of reference, may be slower to accept this interpretation of the feelings both conscious and unconscious at play in counselling training and supervision sessions. They will listen carefully to the suggestion and give it due consideration as they monitor their feelings in the supervision session. This they are trained to do. For the most part we would be sensible not to apply Stoltenberg and Delworth's assertion too broadly and crudely without acknowledging that there are always individual differences at play in the situation described, bringing about differing emphases of experience. On the other hand, this should not lead us to deny, or avoid recognizing, that this is an area of potential abuse.

Elizabeth Holloway (1995, pp. 46–47) discusses these reflections through a research report, which states that: 'the supervisor holds the *"relational control"* [my emphasis] in the [supervision] interaction'. This is undoubtedly true. But the character of the relationship is the key to understanding how the relational control is used. I am advocating a position that recognizes this hierarchical relationship but at the same time denies that it need be oppressive or censoring in the supervisee's experience, especially those working as mature therapists and counsellors in private, independent practice. In my own experience as a supervisor I believe the outcome has been quite the contrary to the suggestion that I have dominated my clients in supervision. But my supervisees would be the best judge of that! My view of the relational approach to supervision is that the exercise is one of common learning, where the supervision session operates to the therapeutic benefit of both participants.

My relational control occurs and is most felt in the structure of the sessions. It occurs at a time when I can best manage to provide time. It occurs on my premises and in surroundings that I have designed and control. The sessions start and end at my prompting within a known timescale. I have a high degree of financial control. The supervisee pays me a fee for the service; although in a number of instances the fee is paid directly or indirectly by an employing organization. I acknowledge the element of control in the relationship and see it as weighted in my favour, but only to a degree, and it is certainly challenged with relative ease.

A legitimate part of relational supervision is when the supervisor emerges as a mentor.

**Example:**

*My telephone rings. It is Clare. She is a counsellor of some skill and sensitivity. She has recently got sessional work in a university as a student counsellor and is dealing with all the problems thrown up by a steady and persistent caseload, and working within a tight timeframe. I am approved by the university as her supervisor. Clare is rather worried. She has been presented with a client: a young male student, who has a grandiose manner and claims great distinction in all his work and hobby pursuits. He appears to have a lot of money. He complains of suffering panic attacks. She is worried and puzzled about this strange combination of super-confidence and intense anxiety and asks me to provide a short consultation on the phone. I am happy to do so. She wonders whether her client is on the verge of a manic-depressive break-down. She has never worked in a mental hospital or within a psychiatric regime and is uncertain of her ground. We go on to discuss the client and her fears, and I offer some information and suggestions as to how she might focus the counselling sessions. In this moment I am her mentor and teacher.*

David Malan (1979, pp. 82–83), in an imaginative reconstruction of the supervision situation, illustrates a situation where the supervisor, drawing upon a deep well of experience, offers an interpretation and statement to the trainee psychotherapist, who is feeling guilty because he feels has been overdirective in the therapy situation. He has dismissed the client's own psychoanalytic speculations as: 'a waste of time, merely intellectualizations'. The supervisor is able to take the trainee closer to the concept of defence and how it manifests itself in the therapy situation as the therapy begins to deepen and becomes more threatening to the client. The lesson is that we are all capable of behaving defensively.

Again, the supervisor is acting as a mentor/teacher. This role is special to the supervision relationship, and, although it may in a broad sense be regarded as therapeutic, it is in other respects importantly different.

Clearly the counselling session has much in common with the psychotherapeutic 'hour'. To this extent we can associate the supervision session with the therapy session. But there are important differences that I am stressing. Most apparent, I believe, is my insistence that the supervisor, as well as getting monetary reward from the sessions, benefits in other ways. The sharing of experience between supervisee and supervisor in this context means that they will be exploring the experience of therapy and counselling clients that are familiar to them both. The emphasis will be upon the how and why of the experience for the superviseor. But, as information and procedures emerge, it is likely that this will throw light on the work of the supervisor herself as a therapist. There occurs mutual, although different, learning. These moments are often openly shared and enjoyed by both parties to the relationship in a manner that would not occur in the counselling and therapy session.

## Example

*My supervisor was discussing a case of a young man, in my care, who suffered from a deeply neurotic disorder that made his life a misery. He was at the local university living a life of almost total solitude. He spent many hours travelling to a nearby town to spend daylight hours in cinemas, where he would sometimes be almost the only patron. He avoided young women and had only slight and superficial relationships with men of his own age. He was a difficult case to handle. So far as discussing his family of origin was concerned he was monosyllabic. I found this very frustrating.*

*My supervisor suddenly grabbed her handbag, opened it and emptied its untidy contents on to the table in front of us. 'Here,' she said. 'Pick up any object to represent members of your family and yourself.' I did as she asked. And then at her prompting placing my object, a very phallic fountain pen, in the middle of the table. I put out the rest of the objects in position of emotional distance to myself. So, the further away I placed them, the more emotionally distant I perceived them to be. We did not pursue the 'sculpt' any further. This was not a therapy session! She grinned at me with pleasure and said, 'Well, you could try something like this to get him going. I picked it up from my old supervisor and its proved very useful on occasions.' And I did. And it did prove to be very useful, and I passed on this elementary piece of psychic prompting to a supervisee the other day. I await his next session with interest.*

In this example the symbolic nature of the chosen objects will not be missed by psychoanalytic psychotherapists. More work might well emerge from observations relating to these objects. But counsellors and others, from other therapeutic disciplines, will quickly move into understanding the significance of the 'distances' chosen by the client in representing family relationships. When I became a psychodramatist (Feasey, 2000), I was pleased to see similar sculpting techniques being used – sometimes by employing the presence of group members, sometimes by using 'found' objects in the drama room – as a means of exploring the dynamics of family life. I did not find the transition to psychodramatic techniques difficult to accommodate to my psychoanalytic position. Although I am sure some others would.

In an earlier chapter I mentioned the coffee or tea I keep on offer. It, too, is an important symbolic statement concerning the relationship in the supervision room. It suggests that a different kind of satisfaction is being pursued than that which occurs in the therapy room. It is common for the supervision session to be 'warmed up', as the psychodramatists say, by an opening exchange of greetings and personal information. The atmosphere is that of a meeting between friendly, appreciative colleagues who are interested in one another and share a range of professional interests. This assumption of a level ground is of great importance, even if it is not entirely supported by the psychic reality of the situation. A supervisee explained that she had a difficult time with a previous supervisor who: 'put on her headteacher's hat when I walked into the room.'

This description supports my assertion that therapy and supervision are concerned not only with being reparative functions but also with 'maintenance'. By this I mean helping to ensure that as therapists and counsellors we achieve a healthy lifestyle in work and in our leisure or domestic life. All too frequently I come across therapists and counsellors who seem entirely absorbed with their work and professional concerns, paying slight attention to their own needs as human beings. I am convinced that supervision has a part to play in helping us to give attention to our own well-being in the general sense of that word. I am not discussing the 'pathological' but rather drawing attention to the necessity for counsellors and therapists, of whatever discipline, to achieve balance and harmony in their lives.

So supervision focuses not only on the work with the presented client or group, but also on the professional work within the life issues of the presenting therapist or counsellor. To this extent it is therapeutic.

### Example

*Sarah was a creative therapist working in a large hospital, within a creative therapy context. She specialised in working with the elderly and worked not only with such patients in the hospital setting, but in the community as well, visiting day centres and homes to see her clients. She was a busy, fulfilled therapist, well respected and appreciated by her clients and employers at the time she came to me for supervision.*

*I was from the beginning concerned with her 'whole practice' as well as individual clients and small groups that she ran. Sarah enjoyed good support from her team leader and line manager, a friendly, talented creative therapist with a strong reputation as a therapist and therapeutic innovator. He supported her coming to me for supervision. We met for a number of years and for the most part Sarah presented as a happy, fulfilled person well balanced between her work responsibilities and her family, which consisted of her husband and their three adolescent children.*

*Then a massive change occurred. The line manager/team leader left. A new leader/manager was appointed, and from the earliest day the relationship between this new manager and Sarah became fractious and competitive. Sarah felt undervalued and unappreciated by the manager.*

*The manager, although trained in creative work, came from another arts discipline, a contrast to the previous manager. He was threatened by Sarah and her well-known success.*

*It was not long before Sarah began to bring her sense of conflict and oppression to the supervision sessions. I did not regard the material as neurotic or 'pathological' and saw my task as helping her sort out, professionally, her place in the new situation: finding ways of being and working that were tolerable to her and afforded at least some satisfaction. After about twelve months she left this post and took up another similar one in a neighbouring district. I provided her with a reference relating to her ability as a creative therapist with a special interest in the needs of elderly clients. She was being helped to maintain her professional life and with it her domestic harmony.*

I cannot believe that this is an exceptional case. The supervisor is especially well placed to evaluate the character and quality of work of her supervisee and is well placed, too, to help the supervisee reflect upon the suitability, or otherwise, of proposed employment.

This aspect of the supervision relationship does not call for in-depth therapeutic exploration. Transferences are mostly open and acknowledged, on both sides, and are unlikely to play an unduly influential role in the supervision exchange. The issues are usually pretty clear to the client concerned, and the task in the supervision session is to arrive at a balanced judgement to which the supervisor contributes as far as her knowledge and judgement allow.

It could be argued that this is broadening the role of the supervisor too far and that the prime and only task of the supervisor is to relate to the clinical relationship of the supervisee to her client. I do not agree with this interpretation. I believe that as the supervisor's role grows and develops, in our definition of its purpose, more space will be allowed for a variety of aspects to the role as we understand it now.

I have used the expression 'whole practice' a couple of times in this book, and before closing this chapter I think it would be helpful to amplify the meaning of this expression. I am thinking of the supervisee and the whole context of her working practice. This would include an appreciation of the size of her private practice, the physical circumstances of the practice, any other work the supervisee may be doing (e.g. sessional work at a clinic, hospital or university), sources of referral, her continuing professional development, financial issues and domestic issues, as far as they are implicated in the professional scene.

To conclude this chapter I feel it is possible to summarize the discussion by stating that the essential difference between the therapy/counselling model and the supervision model rests upon certain simple but definitive statements:

1.  In supervision the relationship is one between colleagues, albeit not necessarily at the same level of professional development. This is never the situation in the therapeutic situation.

2   The responsibilities of supervision are diffuse and many faceted, going beyond the specific concern for the client-therapist relationship, which normally prevails in the therapy situation.

3.  The satisfactions of the supervision relationship are not bounded by the presence of 'transference' in the relationship. In many therapeutic situations the client-therapist/counsellor relationship is strictly boundaried by the therapeutic contract.

4.  The supervision context allows for a dialogue between supervisor and supervisee, which embraces topics and experiences not usually found in the therapeutic/counselling relationship; their treatment is fundamentally different. In this respect the supervisor may be seen as acting as a mentor or as a colleague - roles that are accepted and acknowledged by all concerned in the supervision situation.

5.  Issues of hierarchy and control, while present, are not predominant in the exchange between supervisor and supervisee. In therapy and counselling it is usual for the 'power' balance to rest in favour of the therapist/counsellor.

# Chapter 6
# Ethics in supervision: abuse, prejudice, discrimination, gender, race and class

Petruska Clarkson (1997, p. 28) quotes Fletcher (1996) in the following manner:

> Ethics deals with human relations. Situation ethics puts people at the centre of concern, not things. Obligation is to persons, not to things; to subjects, not objects … the notion of value apart from persons is a 'phantasmagoria'. There are no intrinsic values …

With this insightful statement she enters the world of philosophy and theology, which I will not pursue here.

She then goes on to discuss the nature of egocentric satisfaction (erotic): 'My first and last consideration is myself.' Then what I consider to be the conditional position: 'I will give as long as I receive' and, finally, the altruistic, ethical position: 'I will give, requiring nothing in return.' Understanding and holding on to these distinctions help us to stay close to the notion of ethics in supervision, enabling us to monitor our actions and the actions of our supervisees in an understanding way.

Just a personal observation here I must say, but I was relieved to read 'subjects not objects'. The 'object relations' school of psychoanalysis might well take notice.

In this chapter I am extending the notion of ethics to take into account the many shifting perceptions of what amounts to professional responsibilities, in relation to our clients for therapy, or supervision, in our present time. It is quite obvious, for an older generation of therapists, that the tensions of language and behaviour surrounding the headings I have given above would have seemed rarely to occur. Now it is obvious to all of us in our profession that we are likely to engage through therapy and counselling with sensibilities that are alert and concerned with them. And so I intend to take them into account as I discuss the concept of ethics as relating to the work of a supervisor. We are all accustomed to the basic meaning of an ethical position.

The various professional bodies lay down basic ethical values, which we are required to observe. These are often expressed as rules of behaviour, and they are normally accepted by the members without demure. In the work of a supervisor, however, we are likely to get drawn into the issues that I have outlined above by finding areas of tension in the supervisee concerning their own prejudices, wherever these may lie.

Alternatively, the tensions may be in the client or the organizational context that the supervisee is working with. And let it not be assumed that the supervisor is free of prejudice. All of us have grown up in a society that is deeply prejudicial and where prejudice is encountered in every walk of life.

Indeed, as I write, I am conscious, along with many others, that an earlier spirit of tolerance, acceptance and understanding towards immigrants of all kinds (economic or political) seems to be being eroded in the face of authoritarian challenges by those in power in government throughout the whole of Europe.

I remember, as I write this, the anger I felt when I heard a contemporary politician scapegoating the so-called 'gypsies' in our society. They were described as 'bogus refugees'. I remembered that those unfortunate enough to carry that label in Nazi Germany and Eastern Europe were sent to the death camps. Hundreds of thousands died as a result of deeply felt racism. I can only imagine that the politician concerned was momentarily out of touch with the likely effect of his statement upon those who worked with him or looked to him for political and moral leadership. My own wartime experiences and memories, which included a visit to the Belsen concentration camp shortly after the war, played into the anger that welled up in me.

As supervisors we may find ourselves wittingly or unwittingly feeling prejudice toward a supervisee and even acting on it. So it is an absolute necessity for psychotherapists and counsellors not to assume they are beyond the prejudices of the society of which they are members. The cultural filters that operate so assiduously in passing on dangerous value judgements to the members of society where we were born, grew up and came to adulthood, do not leave us without blemish. No personal therapy or counselling relationship rids us completely of the irrational part of our being that surfaces, in deeply judgmental reactions, towards those about us who are vulnerable to such judgement. The most that we can claim as a profession is that we at least strive to be aware of our own personal susceptibilities in this regard. We need to remain wary of the feelings and effects that may come with them.

For the sake of clarity I intend to treat the subheadings chosen above in separate categories, although I realize that they often appear as a compound of influence in our lives.

## Issues of abuse

Although recognizing that the word 'abuse' is a generic term, which covers all the previous subheadings at the opening of this chapter, I intend here to give it individual consideration within a prescribed range of definition.

Virtually all training bodies counsel supervisors, therapists and trainees to avoid any form of abuse with their clients. It seems quite obvious that this would be a first condition of therapy. But a question arises: 'What amounts to and what is the nature of abuse?' The answer is not always clear.

**Sexual abuse** is the first one that comes to mind for many people. The supervisor who sexually abuses a supervisee is likely to be detected relatively quickly (interpreting sexual abuse here as an unwanted or desired sexual exchange of a physical character between supervisor and supervisee). It is important to realize that, even when a sexual exchange is welcomed by the supervisee, it still acts as a grave impediment to the work of supervision, colouring, as it will, all the other exchanges between the two of them. At the same time it is best to remember that supervisors and supervisees are human and in certain circumstances will feel attracted to one another sexually; they may 'fall in love' and want to make love. In this case the simple answer is to suspend the formal supervision relationship promptly. It is up to the former supervisee to then find another supervisor.

Sexual abuse can also take the form of prejudice towards either gender by the supervisee or supervisor. A supervisee who has experienced hurt at the hands of a therapist/counsellor or previous supervisor, one of the opposite sex, may well bring this hurt to the new supervision relationship. It needs to be recognized and dealt with as soon as possible in the new relationship and a decision taken as to whether the supervision relationship can proceed. There is always the danger that the abuse and hurt will repeat itself in supervision unless the supervisor and supervisee bravely confront the potential harm of the situation.

**Emotional abuse** seems to me to be the most common occurrence that is likely to take place in the supervision relationship. This form of abuse presents itself in many forms and is not always easily detected either by the supervisee or the supervisor concerned. For some time I tolerated a very punitive supervisor, largely because he had been instrumental, at one point, in enabling me to get on my feet as an independent psychoanalytic psychotherapist. My view now is that he was largely unaware at the time of the punitive nature of his supervision. I, too, only became fully aware of the situation some years after leaving him and entering into supervision with someone with a completely contrasting style of working. Should we regard this form of punitive supervision as a form of abuse? At one time I might have argued no. But now I would suggest that it is, and we should become aware of it. Certainly, Kaberry (2000) appears to regard it as such. In her survey, although limited, she identifies a number of counsellors complaining of anxious feelings in the supervision situation, experienced as abuse. But there is a problem of judgement and individual reaction. I would regard myself as a robust psychotherapist, well able to take positive criticism, even when it is quite harshly expressed. But another person might easily feel quite undermined by the level of comment and criticism that I could cope with. The only guide to this dilemma is the way the supervisee feels in the relationship and the degree of freedom that exists to examine, and if necessary redress, the experience in such a way as to free both parties from the abuse that is being suffered.

I have centred the discussion on the issue of sex and criticism, but there are other forms of emotional abuse.

For example, a supervisee may well suffer from **neglect**, and neglect comes in a number of forms. It can be detected in the form of haphazard appointments that may result from last-minute change or cancellations. I have already mentioned, earlier in the book, painful memories of sitting in a corridor waiting for my supervision interview, which I was paying for and which was being delayed in favour of another client. This was a frequent occurrence. I had made a 150-mile round trip for this supervision, and I felt the neglect painfully.

Neglect can take the form of the supervisor not being cognitively or emotionally prepared for the supervisee, not remembering, or refreshing her memory of, the particular circumstances of the supervisee. This may well occur in the training situation when the supervisor is a busy psychotherapist barely finding time in an overworked day to prepare properly for a supervision session with a trainee. More crudely, the neglect may simply take the form of the 'absence' of the supervisor in a literal sense. Or even when a supervisor is present in the physical sense of the word, she may not be present. I remember it being reported to me that a group supervisor was known to 'drop off' during a session. None of the supervisees concerned actually complained.

A very successful, much-sought-after therapist or counsellor may take on such a load of therapy and teaching as to be elusive and absent for lengthy periods of time. The supervisee becomes angry and frustrated but frequently silent, intimidated by the distinction of his supervisor. At a more subtle level it may well be the inferior position of the trainee in the training process makes her easily 'forgotten', hence neglected. Many researchers (Lawton, Feltham, Clarkson, Holloway and Stoltenberg) have established that supervisees report feeling inferior in the supervision process and inhibited from making demands of the supervisor. Certainly, I completely failed to challenge my 'punitive superior' supervisor when I suffered neglect. The truth was that

I was too dependent on his goodwill professionally to incur his wrath through complaining. Who would I complain to anyway? I simply dodged the issue, fearful of the consequences.

Where this sense of 'inferiority' is evident, it is likely to result in a form of emotional abuse. It is more likely to occur in the institutional training situation than in private practice. It should be remembered, too, that apart from the training experience in institutes of psychotherapy, training which occurs in mental hospitals and clinics often takes the form of the supervision of junior clinical staff, either individually or in groups. This is often overlooked in the literature. In my own experience of supervising junior staff, most often nurses, in an NHS mental-health setting I had to get used to a relatively passive response from the supervisees when I did my best to encourage active responses.

However, these nurses were accustomed to a learning situation where questions and challenges were not encouraged. This situation could easily have lead to abusive practice upon the part of the supervisor; it would not be difficult for a sense of inferiority to pervade the sessions where the supervisor becomes the 'expert' and the supervisee the uninformed supplicant. The really sad and trying aspect of this situation was that the nurses concerned, accustomed to their 'passive' position in their training lectures, found it very difficult to take on personal responsibility for their own learning and were 'upset' by the process. I am sure some of them resented me in that situation, feeling I had failed them by failing to provide the nourishment they longed for.

**Prejudice is a form of abuse that is widely condemned in our society but still remains a prevalent practice.**

I am grouping **prejudice** with **discrimination** because the former invariably leads to the latter.

It is a feeling state that may arise in a number of situations but is very often associated with race in our contemporary society. There has been an active anti-racist lobby in existence in the UK since the 1960s, when numbers of ethnic immigrants came from the West Indies to take up jobs in health, transport and service organizations. It would be a mistake to imagine that this was the first immigration to this country; we know that Britain had been a host country to immigrants for many years, especially during the eighteenth and nineteenth centuries. But it would be true to say that this was the first time that colour had been the main identifying feature of large numbers of immigrants. Former immigrants tended to come from Eastern Europe and Russia. Only a few came from Africa or the West Indies. It soon became evident that the issue of colour was becoming significant in society at large and in its many institutions. Prejudice and discrimination were widespread and it was some time before it was seriously challenged.

For example, while living in London in the 1950s, I noticed that it was quite usual for landlords to advertise scarce accommodation with the statement 'no coloureds, no Irish'. The two were commonly figured together.

## Race and ethnicity

Supervisors are just as likely as anyone else in our society to have been brought up in a public atmosphere of prejudice and discrimination. Even where the family situation has worked against such bigotry, we cannot dismiss the effect of long-term cultural dissemination of feelings of prejudice and discrimination. In the mental health services of the UK there has long been a suspicion that black patients have been misdiagnosed to their disadvantage over a long period of time. The labels of 'schizophrenia' and 'psychopathic personality disorder' are devastating. These terms have been applied, all too often, to black patients who present with behaviour and language forms that are unfamiliar to the examining clinician (Fletchman, 1993). Only recently I read a painful account, by a black woman, Donna, of her experience in a counselling situation where she felt even her basic language was not understood by the therapist (*Changes* vol. 18, Winter edition, no. 4. p. 230). This demonstrates that, even when ethnic minorities gain access to psychotherapy and counselling, there are problems. Roy Moodley (1999) mentions a significant presence of dissatisfaction and disenchantment and premature departure from psychotherapy, as reported in current research. I have not come across any specific references to the problem in relation to the influence of the supervisor in such cases, but it must be a significant factor. So the supervisor, in whatever context, needs to be aware of these critical issues as far as they present in her own practice, and in the practice of supervisees.

## Example

*A young, very clever woman of mixed race presented to me for psychotherapy in my private practice. She was very angry at the absence of her black father, who lived somewhere on the North American continent. Her white mother lived locally, and they had a reasonably well-balanced emotional relationship. Her anger was complex. Resenting her father's perceived abandonment of the family, she was, nevertheless, making a powerful attachment to his colour and ethnic origins. She had made a journey to the West Indies to find her black family, her father's family of origin. She had traced him in America and kept up a confrontational, engaged relationship with him. He appeared very proud of her intelligence and very aware of the academic distinction she enjoyed. But he remained unapologetic concerning leaving his English family. He had found another relationship in America and had more children. All black. This made her very, very angry. She despised her mixed-race presentation to the world and wanted to be 'truly black', not half white.*

The point of this example is to illustrate the complexity of the issues of race, culture and colour in the life of young people today in our society. This young woman certainly felt anger towards her father, but she loved him and identified in many ways with his ethnicity. She had a complicated problem of personal identity to struggle with, together with a history of barely acknowledged discrimination and prejudice. Working as she did in a large university, where she was well regarded as a researcher, she had been protected to some extent from the current prejudices of our society. This made it difficult for her to identify the source of some of her feelings of lack of worth and significance.

A supervisor working with a supervisee in such a case needs to be well informed and alert to the many-layered tensions of this situation. It is clearly the duty of a supervisor to look to the well-being of the presented client/patient in all respects. The covert abuse present in the case I have described presents a complex challenge to counsellor and supervisor alike. Having stressed the need for all of us to address our own prejudices, the obvious further issue here is to address the issue of the supervisor. A supervisor who ignores the issue of race in her practice with clients from a different ethnic group may only be hiding her own painful feelings of prejudice in the situation. These clients may be supervisees from ethnic-minority groups or patients/clients in the care of a therapist/ counsellor. In either case the supervisor has a duty to be aware of and responsive to issues of racial prejudice, whether of an active or passive character.

Hilde Rapp (1999) describes a supervisor detecting a somewhat aggressive attitude in a new supervisee when describing and negotiating the supervision contract. She interprets this aggression as fear. In this case the new supervisee is a black woman who felt she had been 'despoiled and rejected' by her last supervisor, who was a white woman. It struck me that Hilde Rapp was describing an experience closely reflective of what I have called 'angry fear'. This was basically a social and political judgement with deep and resounding emotional associations. It is not for the supervisor to dismiss one dimension in favour of the other or to set out to therapize the situation and in the process marginalize the social/political judgements, whether they be a product of the supervisee or her client. The issue of difference needs to be worked upon at two levels in supervision. The example given by Hilde Rapp relates to the immediate relationship of the supervisor to the supervisee, but there is another level where this may be encountered, where the supervisee feels deep resentment coming from a client, in counselling or therapy, and is at a loss as to how to identify it or handle it as a counselling/therapy issue.

## Gender

Although I am well aware of a large amount of professional literature concerning the topic and issues of gender – indeed, there are now whole university studies devoted to gender and its significance in our society – I am nevertheless going to draw mostly upon my own experience of gender consciousness in this part of this chapter.

One of my earliest memories is of feeling grateful to the gods that I had not been born a girl. This memory goes back to when I was about six or seven years old. Somehow I perceived, even at that tender age, that being female was to be placed at a disadvantage.

Even as I write this I hear a report on Radio 4 that the Equal Opportunities Commission is complaining that after twenty-five years of legislation women are still suffering discrimination in virtually all aspects of life. As a child I thought men appeared to have all the fun, all the money, did exciting things, travelled, got good jobs, took physical risks in which there was pleasure, were listened to with respect, exercised authority, were often in charge of serious matters and had control over their destiny and so on and so on. The obvious drawbacks did not strike me at the time.

Like most young boys I had a great attachment to my mother. My father was experienced as a rather distant figure: a postman getting up at some preposterous hour and absent from the household for many hours. Apart from delivering letters he was, too, an excellent gardener who enjoyed his solitude on a large garden plot. This only increased my respect for him. My mother's proximity was greatly enjoyed – I simply loved being with her – but it did not make her gender desirable. Women stop you from doing risky things when you are seven years old. At seven I thought boys were adventurous, girls were timid, mothers controlling and dads essentially more likely to say yes. I also thought that older girls, teenagers, were merely extensions of my mother, ready at every opportunity to stop me from doing anything they considered risky.

The supervisor, in counselling and psychotherapy, needs to appreciate her own developmental experience, from the very beginning of her practice, when working with the feelings of her supervisee and the supervisee's clients.

## Example

*My supervisee was a mature, well-educated professional woman with a long and distinguished history as a counsellor and psychotherapist. A series of chance events led to her being placed as a public representative on what amounted to being a local government health quango. She was an ideal choice. She had a strong background of mental health experience to draw upon. She was independently minded, coherent and lucid in her thought and expression. I was pleased when she reported her appointment during a supervision session.*

*However, it was not long before she was 'in trouble' with a heavily male-dominated group, lead in the main by some fairly senior male authority figures. She wanted an item put on the agenda of the meeting that did not suit 'those in charge'. Ironically, the paid adviser and administrator to this group was a woman. This woman, anticipating her male colleagues' disapproval, attempted to block the item being put on the agenda for the next meeting.*

*To everyone's surprise and dismay my client refused to take no for an answer and conducted a brief but energetic campaign to get her voice heard. This was the beginning of a continued struggle within the committee for her to establish her role and gain respect as a committee member, which, eventually, she did.*

*Of course, no one could prove the discrimination was aimed at her as a woman, or whether there was any actual discrimination at all, but she had a need to explore these issues in supervision and did so with my support.*

Much of this material was brought to the supervision session and together we tried to sort out what was reasonable and unreasonable in the situation. She felt safe and free in supervision to examine her own 'agenda', as it were, in a non-judgemental situation where she could take risks and be heard. She could listen with less tension than might have been the case with someone outside the supervision room. This is an instance where I was involved in supervising what I have described earlier as the 'whole practice' of my client, which concerns itself not only with patient/client issues but also with other relevant matters beyond the therapy room.

Of course, my perceptions of femaleness at the age of seven have been radically revised with time, and I would now regard myself as a 'failed feminist'. Failed in the sense that I cannot hope to entirely escape the influence of my early years in respect of this issue. There is still present a little determined boy who is glad that he is a boy. The foolishness rests with the notion of being glad not to be a woman. And yet it lingers. I suspect there are, too, many women who regret being women, although in our PC days of censorship this would be a feeling that would not be too easy to own up to and express. The drawbacks of being female in most respects are all too obvious. Most women get paid less than men, even when doing the same or comparable jobs; they often find it difficult to get work promotion; most women do most of the chores at home; women bear children, usually with pain; most women who are mothers do most of the childcare; most women suffer small discriminations in everyday life without any acknowledgement that this is happening. Women have complex bodily functions exclusive to their sex to deal with. And so on. I shall not labour this description.

In supervision it becomes evident quite quickly that female supervisees, especially those in training, are subject to emotional influences that may be directed at them in a form and intensity that does not occur so often, or in the same manner, to men. The example given illustrates the situation outside the training programme, but I have supervised a number of women in training who have quite obviously experienced an element of discrimination in respect to their gender.

### Example

*Jane was a trainee in an integrated psychotherapy training course. She was a bright, talented and committed trainee. In supervision she was most committed and regular in her attendance and rewarding in the level of work she was prepared to undertake. Difficulties arose when a male trainer left her course and a woman from an analytical background entered the course as a senior tutor. The new tutor seemed punitive and demanding of my supervisee. She rarely praised, was quick to find fault and was disparaging of elements of the course that were not primarily psychoanalytical in character.*

*My supervisee was dismayed to find herself in a situation she was not accustomed to. She admitted in our discussions that she had been something of a 'favourite' of the former male tutor. She sensed he 'fancied' her. She found him attractive too but made no conscious sexual overtures to him. But she did enjoy his favours and admitted she was always glad to spend time with him over a cup of coffee between teaching sessions. This had provoked a certain amount of teasing from other course members. Now it was as if the new woman tutor was putting her in her place. Maybe she was aware of the interest her predecessor had shown in Jane and suspected a sexual component leading to favouritism.*

This is a somewhat complex situation, and in the supervision sessions I was careful not to appear to blame either my female client, her former male tutor or the new female tutor. But gender tension certainly existed in the situation, as described by the supervisee. She eventually came to recognize that there were elements of discrimination in her favour in the first tutorial relationship, but a price had been paid associated with her sex and the sexual fantasies that had been expressed by other trainees on the course. She decided to monitor the new tutorial relationship carefully to see whether she was being more critically dealt with than the other trainees, especially the women. I am not for a moment suggesting that male trainees never get themselves involved in situations of peer rivalry and jealousy, but the overtly sexually attractive woman is more likely to become susceptible to such stressful experiences, whether it comes from men or women. Our sexual attractiveness to others, or lack of it, plays a strong part in professional relationships.

Whilst the example given above relates to the supervisee in her training situation, it could easily apply to the appearance of the supervisor. It may not appear to be specifically sexual. Sometimes convention or social expectation plays a significant part in our judgement of others. Habitually I do not wear a tie and on one occasion this was commented upon, jokingly, by a somewhat serious, conventional woman supervisee. Readers may recall Freud had some interesting things to say about jokes and humour!

I am focussing upon the work of the supervisor in relation to issues that are not, in the first instance, concerned with the supervisee's clinical practice.

Issues of perception are, in my view, still an essential aspect of the supervision task. Obviously, the issue of gender will come up sharply in the clinical situation and my client, drawing upon this tutorial experience, applied the learning to the therapy relationship, where she became distinctly aware of attempts to 'seduce' her by attractive male clients. She realized all was not transference, and she held a direct responsibility for what emerged sexually in the therapy relationship. There was a need for me, too, as her supervisor, to accept that she was a sexually attractive woman. Indeed, I knew it was important to keep in focus her unconscious pleasure and response to both men and women who were attracted to her looks and personality.

At a nearer clinical level, all supervisors know that women frequently get verbally attacked by clients in therapy. The 'Madonna and whore syndrome' is well known to counsellors and therapists alike. The supervisee, when a woman, is quite likely to be on the receiving end of such projections, receiving punishment in the form of emotional abuse for the failures and difficulties of a client's life in dealing with significant female figures. The depriving or punishing mother is another common fantasy figure likely to occur in counselling and therapy. This is all too common and an inexperienced supervisee may well be bemused and hurt by such behaviour, and seek the supervisor's support. The task of the supervisor is to assist in clarifying these situations as they occur, not only to the ultimate benefit of the patient/ client, but the supervisee as well. It is interesting to note that sometimes supervisees make it absolutely clear that they want to work with either a man or woman supervisor. If they are in private practice, this is usually easily accommodated, but in institutional practice difficulties can more easily arise in this respect.

## Class

Gender and racial prejudice are not the only commonly experienced form of social prejudice experienced in our society. Prejudice about class is still a significant feature of contemporary British society. It pervades all our institutions and nowhere more than in the field of psychiatry, psychotherapy and counselling (Pilgrim, 1997). Psychoanalytic psychotherapy has been especially guilty of promoting a view that the uneducated, so-called 'concrete thinking', working-class members of our society cannot, in general, benefit from introspective psychotherapy (Feasey, 1999). Generally speaking, I have found those trained in person-centred counselling less prejudiced in this respect. This is especially so in counselling in GP practices, where counsellors are presented with a broad social spectrum of the local population.

The prejudice that attaches itself to class means that again, as with black people, working-class clients may never be offered therapy or counselling within a psychiatric context because it is believed it would be a waste of time and energy, and ultimately ineffective. Often such clients are described as lacking psychological awareness and have no language of self-description or relationships. A number of authors have addressed this issue (Kovel, Coltart, Storr, Dryden, Pilgrim, Brown and Pedder). Of course, if you are working class and black, you are in a very bad way! Abusive neglect and superficial judgement arising from cultural issues can lead to the overuse of drugs and electrotherapy as the therapy of choice in dealing with emotional problems that rarely respond positively to such crude medical applications. I had personal experience of this situation when a close relative became mentally ill and was admitted as an in-patient and remained in hospital care for many months. Apart from being a witness to her suffering, which was very painful, I was struck by the population of working-class patients patiently and passively receiving ECT and drugs, as the therapy of psychiatric choice. Needless to say, the patients had little say in this matter. No other approach to dealing with what were often deeply placed emotional problems was considered.

In the case of my relative, an elderly lady, now deceased, she was inappropriately treated with a series of ECT shocks, which triggered an exceptionally distressing psychotic experience, where she imagined the ward she was in was on fire. She was trapped in an adult cot under restraint. My wife and I used our influence, energy and ability to communicate with the health professionals to bring this disastrous treatment to a swift end.

The absurdity of these generalizations about working-class men, women and children was brought home to me when I worked as a psychotherapist at an NHS hospital in the north of England. In a modified day therapeutic community the majority of our patients were underprivileged, often unemployed, working-class men and women. Many of them had been referred to us because they were regarded as untreatable by the local doctors, psychiatrists and social workers!

Our research programme that followed up the treatment of these patients in our community suggested strongly that the group/community psychotherapeutic approach we employed was relatively successful. The evidence was found in the falling off of self-referrals to the local GPs by discharged patients from our unit.

These research findings encouraged us, and our supervisors became well equipped with information concerning the efficacy of the group psychotherapeutic approach, within a day therapeutic community. It is incumbent on supervisors, working with counsellors and psychotherapists of all disciplines, to be aware of the manner in which class prejudice and discrimination operates against the well-being of the client.

Let it not be thought that it is only the prejudiced psychiatrists working within a medical model who display prejudice towards working-class patients. I have already mentioned the manner in which psychotherapists can suggest the 'concrete thinking' of working-class patients, which precludes them from being able to seek understanding and relief through abstract or 'philosophical' explanation, excludes certain patients from analytic treatment. I notice it is becoming more commonplace now for such patients to be dismissed by psychotherapists with the label of 'borderline personality', 'personality disordered', 'schizoid personality type' or 'psychopathic disordered' and thus unsuitable for the application of psychotherapy. In researching my article (Feasey, 1998) 'Will it or Won't it Work?' I found texts that almost drifted into absurdity as they found more and more classes of patients unsuitable for psychoanalytic psychotherapy. What appeared to be a unifying feature of these patients was their social origins.

I can hear some of my readers complain: 'I would never discriminate against anyone on the basis of their colour or class.'

Would that were true! I argue that we are all members of a society in which there is evidence of entrenched prejudice. We breathe it in like the air around us. We cannot ever escape its influence on us as supervisiors, therapists and members of society.

# Chapter 7
# Difference, disability, political belief and religion

## Politics

I can hear some counsellors and therapists say: 'But this is all politics! Therapy and counselling have nothing to do with class discrimination and race issues.'

The issues of class and race are political issues. I argue that it is our prime duty to become aware and remain aware of the influence of politics in our professional lives. We are all political creatures and must be if we are to be responsible citizens in our society. Every five years or so we are called upon to vote for a political party and, despite much cynicism, most of us do. Party political programmes have a direct impact upon the health services of the UK, both private and public, physical and mental health services. If a potential supervisor told me that she was completely free of prejudice or political allegiance, I would look elsewhere for support.

## Example

*Joan came for her first supervision appointment. I showed her into my pleasant therapy/sitting room and asked her to make herself comfortable while I fetched my notes. It is my custom to allow the clients a short time in the supervision room to familiarize themselves with the atmosphere, to make themselves physically and emotionally comfortable and to prepare inwardly for the session about to start. I left the room. Joan did not sit down. She wandered about the room looking at the pictures on the wall and the furniture, satisfying her curiosity. Then she looked at a large bookcase I have in the room with about 400 paperback books displayed. She glanced at the titles. And I think she was immediately interested. She was looking into my life. I returned. She sat down and so did I. I began to prepare my note pad. She spoke: 'Well, you are an old lefty, aren't you?' And then she grinned at me in a friendly way. She continued: 'Quite a collection of Left Book Club editions; how did you find them?'*

In this example I am simply pointing out how sensitive and alert our super-visees may be to any clues we leave lying around about our religious, political or philosophical beliefs. In this case Joan was very happy with what she had discovered. But she may well have been disconcerted at what I had revealed through my bookshelf. My view is that as long as we remain, as supervisors, aware of the need to be honest, open and thoroughly professional in our work with our client supervisees, then for the most part, any uneasiness about our belief systems being markedly different from our supervisees' may be properly handled. In my early training days I was in group analysis with a conductor who, I knew, was a keen supporter of the radical wing of the Labour party, an 'old Labourite' he would be known as today. He never betrayed his political position in the group or in the teaching seminars that he sometimes gave, but I felt a certain comfort in knowing that we would see eye to eye on most matters of social policy, including the mental health services of the day. I still remember his white face on the day that Harold Wilson resigned.

It seems to me sad that many counsellors and therapists I meet in a profes-sional setting are reluctant to admit spontaneously to a 'political' position. It is as if the day they entered the world of psychotherapy they became politically neutered. Quite unnecessarily in my view. It is a matter, most of the time, of keeping boundaries alive and properly placed, according to the supervision situation, and not attempting to be less than a mature citizen with social and political responsibilities (Pilgrim, 1997). On the whole I think that counsellors find this easier to achieve than many psychoanalytic psychotherapists who sometimes tend to carry their professional anonymity into their social position.

## Difference and disability

It appears that people with disability are rarely found in the profession of psychotherapy and counselling. Why this is so I do not know. I can only imagine that there is some form of discrimination at work, which discrimin-ates against the recruitment and training of disabled people as therapists, counsellors and supervisors. I have worked with disabled clients from a range of disability backgrounds. What I have learned from this is that my clients have frequently had to struggle hard to obtain equal opportunities in a cultural climate where they are often marginalized. This has two levels of impact on the work of a supervisor. First, if we do have a disabled supervisee, we need to be informed about her world, her values and her experiences of being disabled in the world of the so-called 'normal'. Second, if the disabled person is the supervisee's client, we have a special duty towards that client to ensure that her special needs are met in therapy and not treated as a side issue or, even worse, pathologized in the relationship with the therapist.

Sometimes the presenting feeling in the therapy and, consequently, in the supervision is angry fear, refered to earlier in this text.

I have experienced this angry fear in the two former clients already mentioned, one of whom suffered a physical impairment and became wheelchair bound. The other was deaf. With both I had to find a way of 'being' that respected their particular impairment issues without patronizing or treating them as being other than normal human beings. In both cases I had to deal with their expectations, some of which were vested in the anger they felt, as they experienced discrimination of every description. Another client, from the north of England, heard my southern accent as 'posh', middle class and thus alienating. She left therapy, precipitously, before we could get to grips with the issues concerned. Some of these issues were to do with transference feelings towards me as an older man and some were to do with class issues, where she sometimes felt diminished, angry and helpless.

Projections from these clients were very powerful and controlling and a powerful struggle took place in the therapy to maintain and develop the relationship along therapeutic lines. These were particular incidents within my professional practice and were specific to the people concerned; however, any 'difference' from the culturally bound stereotypes of normality of our multicultural society can impinge upon the supervisory relationship and therapy.

Sometimes a supervisee may be manifesting resentment towards a client where feelings of 'loss of worth' are occurring in the supervisee in their relationship with the client. Perhaps the loss of worth being experienced in the counselling/therapy relationship is impinging upon the therapist in such a way as to engage the therapist's anger, fear, repugnance, jealousy or sense of inferiority.

I discussed fear in the psychotherapeutic relationship with a clever, sophisticated, gay psychotherapist recently. He admitted that every now and again he realized that he presented as a threatening and fearful figure to insecure heterosexual men and women, some of them therapy colleagues. In some of these colleagues there was a simplistic, inaccurate, fearful identification of homosexuality with paedophilia. This threatening judgement produced fear in those making this judgement and anger in him, as he realized he was being identified in this way. As I write this a political scandal has broken out, where a gay man in public office is under intense scrutiny from the press and may well be feeling he is suffering discrimination, partly as a result of his sexual orientation. Often fear and anger in the heterosexual self towards homosexual men or women is a reflection of anxiety about sexual identity or the product of anxiety about sexual/social performance. There are many other reasons for homophobia, and a good supervisor is likely to become especially alert to their presence as anxiety enters the consulting room of supervision.

As far as physical disability is concerned, the supervisee and the supervisor need to recognize that such a condition can sometimes threaten the usual arrangements for therapy. I recall being somewhat shocked that the deaf client had to reorganize the seating arrangement in my therapy room and set about doing so in order that he could lip-read me with greater ease. It came as a shock to the system. At first I was simply a bit disconcerted, but I also had to recognize that we were quickly thrown into a close and engaged relationship, in which there were strong elements of fear, anger and competition. I had a lot to learn about the culture of the deaf community and how forceful it is. My deaf client had come with a host of assumptions about psychoanalytic psychotherapy, and I think he found my energy in the therapy session surprising.

The wheelchair user had to be supported as he used crutches to get to his special car from my house after a therapy session had finished. I held his arm in a supportive way and saw him safely down the few steps leading out of my house. So we had physical contact. The counsellor is likely to be much more at ease with these arrangements than the psychoanalytic psychotherapist. It is unfortunate that the training of psychoanalytic therapists can sometimes produce a rigidity of response towards clients that impacts negatively on persons suffering a disability. Also it needs to be borne in mind that the image of the speechless, silent psychoanalyst has impinged upon the popular consciousness; so the actuality of a therapist may come as a shock to a new client. This was certainly true in the case I have just described.

It also needs to be borne in mind that many people feel very disturbed by the presence of disability in others. Sometimes powerful primitive feelings of disgust, flowing from anxiety, impinge upon what is felt towards people with apparent disabilities. I recall a child who would shrink back in fear from any person exhibiting any sort of physical disability. Out shopping she would insist on her mother taking her across the road if there was any likelihood of a public encounter of this sort on the footpath. Someone with an arm in a sling would fill her with fear. Her liberal, well-educated parents found this behaviour puzzling. They were completely baffled by their daughter's behaviour.

A supervisor working with a supervisee who works with disabled clients must be aware of the possibility of totally irrational responses in the therapy and supervision setting. It strikes me, too, that I have met only one disabled supervisor, although, no doubt, others exist.

Most of us can recall how the 'different' child was persecuted in the playground at school, especially in the junior school where the young children behave with open discrimination against those who appear not to conform to the standards they hold up as being normal. They may do this with an innocent intent, not realizing the damage that may be being caused. Both the damaging and the being damaged aspect of such behaviour can live with people throughout their lives; it is the essence of bullying, hence persecutory behaviour. It is essential that, when sensing such a background of persecution, we in our supervisory role check it out carefully with our supervisees. The rule here seems to be not to assume anything but to remain open to such possibilities of persecution and to respect the supervisee's account and evaluation. We must always remember, too, that our energy as supervisors may sometimes be interpreted as a form of attack and persecution. It is not always easy to be sure which is which. We must be ready to confront that interpretation openly and honestly in the scrutiny of ourselves, addressing it in the supervision dialogue. A highly fictional account of the phenomenon of difference, scapegoating and persecution with near-tragic consequences is found in *Lord of the Flies* by William Golding (1954).

If we are working in the supervisory role within an institutional framework, e.g. a hospital or clinic, GP surgery or training organization, we have to be aware that our institution may well exhibit prejudice against people seen as 'different' within the organization. This difference may be seen as a difference of sexual identity, in race and colour, in educational background and achievement, in status and professional training/qualification. Working as a non-medical psychotherapist within a predominantly medical setting, such as a hospital or GP practice, may be the setting for the worst experience of this kind of behaviour.

I was working in a large NHS mental hospital and became a victim of the most obvious professional rivalrous behaviour, which I was quite incapable of rectifying in any way. In the two years of working as a psychotherapist in the hospital, on a sessional basis, I never found or was allocated a secure, continuously available therapy space. I tried writing to the hospital manager on at least six occasions, requesting an interview to discuss the situation. He never acknowledged a single letter. It was only at a meeting with peers when I sought supervision on this issue, that I finally found the courage to admit defeat and leave the employ of the hospital. A friendly consultant psychiatrist, psychoanalytically trained, said to me: 'Don, without a powerful medical mentor in that hospital you will never survive.'

He was right. Without his intervention I might have gone on punishing myself for a lot longer, simply by failing to leave.

Sometimes it is the business of the supervisor to be blunt and directive in an assessment of a situation, to articulate it clearly for the supervisee to hear and respond to.

Many immigrants to the UK, coming with first-class professional training from other countries in Europe find that they are regarded as 'inferior' or not sufficiently qualified by their counterparts in this country. The British Psychological Society is particularly demanding in this respect. As supervisors we must test this judgement in ourselves to gauge whether there is any proper evidence for this conclusion when working with a colleague. At least three of the most respected therapists I have worked with were trained in Europe: one in Sweden, one in Hungary and the other in Poland. The latter, a senior clinical psychologist from Warsaw, had to jump through very challenging hoops to satisfy The British Psychological Society of his competence, which, with great patience, he did. The Hungarian, another qualified and experienced clinical psychologist/therapist, had to virtually 'start again' in acquiring UK qualifications in order to be seen as a competent psychotherapist in the UK. In all these instances I had warm relationships with the people concerned. But I wonder whether I would have found it so easy to accept their 'foreignness' if I had experienced them as being unfriendly, defensive and unattractive, and perhaps angry with the way they were received professionally in the UK. Our subjective selves must always be reckoned with.

Paradoxically, when working as a trainer in Russia shortly before the collapse of Communism, I found myself overvalued by Russian trainees. The feeling that 'experts' from the West had information and experience of which the trainees had been starved, and were necessarily vastly 'better' equipped as psychotherapists, prevailed. The reality was that only part of this was true and the Russians had therapy experience which I valued and was new to me. I found this to be true in other parts of Eastern Europe that I visited. In my supervision role with them I had to remain alert to quite subtle moments of self-deprecation in my trainees, who found it difficult to value themselves sufficiently in the training situation with this 'expert' from the West.

Working abroad, in my experience, tended to activate a certain grandiosity in me. I felt valued in a way that I did not experience 'at home' in Britain. I do not think this feeling was peculiar to me. On the contrary, I think a great deal of the attraction of working abroad is the experience of being honoured, when that honour is not so apparent from those who are closer and more familiar to us. There is a special lesson to be learned from this for supervisors. Supervisors, whether working at home or abroad, may well become overvalued. They will inevitably attract 'followers', who will idealize them and proselytize on their behalf. So it is important that someone, preferably the supervisor herself, will point out that the empress has no clothes!

I conclude with a brief word concerning belief and religious attachment.

I have revealed a certain political and social position that I hold. I do not apologise for this. Indeed, I think it is a sign of maturity in a human being to have reached certain benign political, religious and moral conclusions in life. Freud was a political and social conservative although paradoxically he was advancing a revolutionary view of mental health. As he was growing up in Central Europe revolutionary doctrines from the left and right were sweeping through the society of which he was a member, but he seems to have stood aside and was actually critical of left-wing exhortations. Paradoxically, he and his family became victims, as Jews, of extreme right-wing terror in the form of Nazism, and he was forced to flee Vienna in 1938. Some family members stayed behind in Vienna and were murdered in the concentration camps.

His social views were sometimes difficult to understand. He seems to have had no time at all for birth control, apart from abstinence! It appears that he became sexually inactive in his middle age. At this point of his life condoms were available and were helping to curtail the spread of venereal diseases, as well as preventing unwanted pregnancies. We know that Freud spoke with dread and anger about these diseases, but he did not welcome prophylactics. At the same time he was often attacked by orthodox medicine and puritans for his 'advanced' views on the place of sexuality in our lives. As far as being a Jew was concerned, he adopted an atheistical attitude, although I think he was always respectful of Jewish culture and history. Freud was clearly a paradoxical figure, sometimes difficult to understand. Like Freud I am an atheist, but having been brought up in a conventional C of E family, singing with great enthusiasm in the choir of an Anglo-Catholic church, I remain respectful of the place of all religions and ritual in our society and the world at large. But I am no admirer of religious excess, in whatever form.

Carl Rogers was quite obviously progressive in his ideas and statements and behaved, as he advocated, in the spirit of warmth and 'unconditional regard' towards those about him: an attractive figure. On the whole counsellors are not burdened as much as psychoanalytical psychotherapists with the idea of complete self-effacement in the therapy situation. Of course, in reality this is a matter of appropriateness, but the wall of silence and neutrality that some psychotherapists consistently employ seems to me a misinterpretation, even a serious distortion, of what is required in working with transference feelings from clients and supervisees. Such a position of 'absence' could be interpreted in some instances as defensive, the therapeutic stance being experienced as a mark of unavailability: the therapist concerned being seen as a cold and remote figure, lacking in any true empathy; even a person aloof from the day-to-day concerns of our society.

I have discussed politics with a large 'P'. But psychoanalysis has always been riven with disputes and rivalries. This has been less true for those who come from a counselling culture. I notice that many of the new institutes that have been set up to train psychotherapists quickly adopt defensive postures in relation to other bodies working in the same field. Indeed, sometimes they appear to claim exclusive rights over the training and professional life of their graduates. Supervisors may encounter this when they are disallowed from working with a supervisee who is from a different training organization than their own. This will be particularly felt when the supervisor is, like myself, self-employed, an independent practitioner. One can only hope that the new world of therapy and counselling will not go the way of the early splits in the world of psychoanalysis, where the Freudians, Jungians, the Adlerians and the Kleinians moved away from each other disputationally, as theoretical differences occurred. The Jungians were especially subject to this splitting. The breaking away from the UKCP of the psychoanalysts is an unhappy premonition. All these political events, with a small 'p', impact upon supervisors. They, especially, are susceptible to the impact of dispute, as they are often seen as the main bearers of the theoretical orthodoxy of their affiliated training body.

Apart from differences in political positions, the supervisee who presents a radically 'different' world view from our own as supervisor presents a problem. This is particularly true in the area of powerful religious beliefs, whether these beliefs come from the mainstream of religious ideas or from radical, fringe religious attachments. With the presence of new immigrant populations in our society has come a rich variety of religious ideas and practices. Some of these immigrants will enter the world of psychotherapy and counselling as practitioners and will be encountered by supervisors who hold markedly different beliefs. In this book I cannot lay down any rule of behaviour or judgement except to say that we need to be aware and responsive, as individuals and as a profession, to the challenge of these belief systems in our work and to respond appropriately. Final judgements in this area must be left to the supervisor and her supervisee in the context of their relationship and practice. But it should not be regarded as a failure if the supervisor turns away a possible supervisee client on the grounds of professional incompatibility based on conflicting belief systems.

This situation is even further confounded when the supervisee is attempting to work with a client who holds distinctive beliefs that she, as the therapist, not only cannot share but actually disapproves of within her own belief system. She turns to the supervisor for help who is then put into a position of conflict, which has to be resolved as honestly as possible within both the supervisor and the relationship with the supervisee.

As readers will have deduced, most of these complicated and interwoven arguments come back to the integrity and honesty of supervisee and supervisor alike. They both have to work within the spirit of trust in one another. There is no final replacement for those virtues in the practice of psychotherapy and counselling supervision.

I make no apology to the reader for giving as much space as this to topics that might strike some therapists and counsellors as not immediately relevant to the work of supervision and the experience of being a supervisee. My own view is that as therapists and counsellors we are in no different position to other citizens in society, and, indeed, there rests upon us a special responsi-bility to hold our beliefs up to self-scrutiny from time to time so as to ensure that our professional position of non-judgementalism is sincerely and properly upheld. A recent publication, *This is Madness* (Newnes, Holmes and Dunn, 1999), is a refreshingly radical challenge to any complacency we may feel about the place of psychiatry and the treatment of mental illness in our present society. It is obvious, too, that psychotherapy and counselling are often uneasy companions to psychiatric practice and values. David Pilgrim and Lesley Hitchman (1999, pp. 190–193) point out in this challenging book that the present Government stresses public safety rather than individual rights in the matter of mental health practice. It is obvious that mental health issues are currently political and are likely to remain so. Supervisors need to take note and on occasions not to be fearful of taking a stand, whether it be moral or political, in favour of those in our society who may be experiencing damaging discrimination.

# Chapter 8
# Listening, understanding and interpreting

In this chapter I shall be examining the way that techniques of supervision are encountered within the relational approach to supervision.

Sometimes techniques of therapy and counselling are divorced from the relationship, as if they can be learned independently and applied without taking any real account of the therapeutic context in which they are applied. Some years ago I was asked by a large health authority to provide an introductory course in counselling skills to nurses who were making the transition from their traditional hospital-based roles to work in the community. I agreed on condition that I would have complete control of the design, content and application of the course. On the first day of the course many of the nurses, all women, came dressed in complete and traditional uniform, despite the fact that I had asked them in advance to come wearing whatever casual clothes they pleased. A number of them brandished notebooks and obviously looked around them for a flip chart. They had no anticipation of experiential learning. The skills they had come to learn were, they thought, likely to be given to them in the form of lecture notes, followed by a question-and-answer session. They were to learn otherwise.

The venue I was using was more like a dance or drama studio than a lecture room. My intention was to involve these nurses very quickly in interactive exercises that would enable them to take a look at the way they related to each other and their individual roles in the training process. This was to be the warm-up to examining their roles in the community, the way they were likely to be perceived by their patients and the experience, new to most of them, of entering the domestic settings of their patients. I was using creative dramatherapy techniques as a means of bringing energy and emotional experience to their learning. This energy would be integrated into their need to learn how to listen to and communicate with their patients and at the same time remain aware of themselves in this, for most of them, new and demanding situation. At a later stage in the course I introduced drama games and video observation, with good sound recording facilities, to expand the learning situation.

The aim of this approach was to ensure that the techniques of counselling skills did not get separated from the need of these nurses to experience the emotional content of their roles, both for themselves and their patients. The assumption was that they would be entering a therapeutic situation. Simple psychodramatic exercises are useful, as in role-reversal techniques, to enable clinical workers to experience and better understand how it feels to be the patient.

Supervisors in their professional roles, which will always include an element of teaching, are faced with a situation where sometimes they will be encouraged to separate this aspect of their activity from other parts of their role, which are more embedded in the culture of therapy. Just as the newly arriving nurses interpreted the training as belonging to the skills element of their work and came in uniform, with their notebooks at the ready, so supervisors when moving, perhaps consciously, into a teaching mode will be tempted to 'chalk and talk', as the teachers say. There is now evolving a literature of supervision training that attempts to analyse and set out, in almost diagrammatic form, the content and skills of supervision. Michael Carroll (1995) sets out a list of supervision 'tasks' and identifies them as follows:

1. the relationship task
2. the teaching/learning task
3. the counselling task
4. the monitoring task
5. the evaluation task
6. the consultative task
7. the administrative task.

He then goes on to set up research projects on these tasks and to attempt to integrate his findings into training courses for supervisors.

I have no objection, in principle, to these schematic attempts at defining the role and tasks of the supervisor; indeed, I am sure that they are useful in enabling supervisors and supervisees to think more clearly about their respective roles. But my emphasis, as stated earlier, is to place the role and tasks into a relational context.

## Listening and watching

I find myself reflecting upon the way in which the culture of counselling and psychotherapy finds itself replicated in the supervision relationship and one of the principal elements of the culture is that of *focussed listening*. The act of listening in a concentrated and focussed way is never more witnessed than when it is employed in counselling and therapy, especially in the individual session. Fortunately, the training of counsellors and psychotherapists virtually always incorporates experiences of focussed listening by the training therapist or counsellor. We all learn to emulate this from this first example and understand its importance. As trainees we come to understand that this is an exceptional experience. There are very few other areas of life in which we shall receive such undivided attention. The accompanying feature of this attention is listening to understand, suspending all judgement until the meaning of the communication in the therapy and counselling situation is clear. Sometimes this means delaying a comment or explanation or interpretation until clarity is possible (Malan, 1979, pp. 81-90).

Implicated with the task of focussed listening is the idea of watching. In counselling and therapy there is a strong agenda of watching. We are watched by our clients, we are under scrutiny and it has to be assumed that our presence is observed and interpreted by the client throughout the session. Similarly, we watch our clients and both consciously and unconsciously interpret their action in the therapy and counselling room (Renton, 1981).

In my view not enough attention is given to this in the training situation. I often ask my supervisees what their clients look like, how they dress, sit and walk in the counselling situation. Certain aspects of the client's appearance and behaviour impact upon the therapist, often without acknowledgement between therapist and client. It is important that the supervisor provides an arena of freedom where such material can be explored with a degree of ease.

When the supervisee enters our room for supervision, our watching tells us a great deal about what she is likely to be bringing with her and her feelings about the coming session. She scrutinizes us, at some level picks up our attitude towards her, our degree of preparation and interest in her presence and what she requires. Much of this is conveyed through our body language long before we speak. For a comprehensive discussion of non-verbal communication I still refer to Argyle (1969 and 1970), who maintains that much that is taboo verbally is revealed in non-verbal communication. So the supervisor is required to maintain a level of observation of NVC that reflects not only on the supervisee's client but also on the communication of the supervisee herself as she works in the supervision room. Much of the writing about NVC is concerned with the observation of the individual in a social context or in the dyadic situation. There is not so much consideration of NVC within the group situation. I shall be expanding my discussion of groups later in the book.

So *listening* is associated with *watching* leading to *understanding*. Just as we watch at different levels so we listen at different levels. A mature and experienced supervisor is likely to carry out all these functions simultaneously, without much conscious awareness of the process, assimilating the information and using it in the supervision session.

## Understanding and interpretation

The surface dialogue may well contain all the material we need as a supervisor to work effectively. And much of the time this is true. But there are times when our listening will pick up anxiety and distress, or a non-specific energy in the session, which may not be revealed in the surface words being used by the supervisee. This immediately raises issues about the nature of the supervision relationship; it appears, in this instance quoted, that we are nudging towards a counselling or therapeutic shift in the relationship. The borderline is a fine one but nevertheless real.

A prime requirement of the supervisor, having given full attention to the supervisee, is to try to *understand* the nature of what is being revealed. The counsellor will probably attempt to understand, through the process of empathetic identification and reflection, together with remaining alert to her own experience from which to draw material in order to assist the client supervisee. The psychoanalytic supervisee will listen with an awareness of the importance of the unconscious world of the client and the manner in which the unconscious communicates. This may well lead to a reflection or a comment or, more rarely, an interpretation. At this point I wish to state my own view of the term 'interpretation'. It often gives rise to irritation in other therapists and counsellors, or lay people, who accuse the psychoanalytical therapist of 'telling' the client the meaning of her experience.

I would stress that this is not my understanding or practice. I do not 'tell' any of my clients the meaning of their experience, whether they be clinical clients or supervisees. Rather my approach is to draw the attention of the client to the statement, attitude or feeling and ask them to consider its deeper meaning, or perhaps its meaning behind the obscurity of its presentation. The client is asked to explore and discover a layer of meaning within the dialogue for themselves. This does not mean that I do not contribute towards the discussion. But I learned from my former tutors at the West Midlands Institute many years ago the value of the words 'perhaps', 'maybe' and 'may I suggest'.

The aim of such reflection or interpretation is to bring meaning to the dialogue so that understanding is achieved and shared between supervisor and supervisee. It has always to be borne in mind that the understanding achieved must be meaningful to the supervisee, not merely to the supervisor. Otherwise nothing has been achieved of any value.

### Example

*Pamela, a very experienced psychotherapist, presents a patient she is working with at a local hospital. The patient presents material from her life experience that speaks of chaos, impulsiveness, thoughtlessness and naïvety. My supervisee sits in front of me complaining that she feels deskilled by the overwhelming nature of the accounts given to her by her client. She resents much of the material and admits to thinking about her on the way to the supervision session, describing her patient to herself as a 'bloody stupid woman'. Pamela talks about being unable to hold a psycho-analytic framework of reference with this patient, and I, too, begin to feel oppressed by the confusion that Pamela is describing, confusion that not only resides in her client but in Pamela as well. Now it is beginning to affect me! Not only do I begin to feel irritation with the patient we are discussing but also I am beginning to wish we could move on to a different case presentation and am getting a bit annoyed with Pamela for staying with the 'tiresome' woman patient.*

*Suddenly I have a memory and from it a feeling that helps to ease the matter for me. I try it out with Pamela. 'You know all this chaos and confu-sion and impulsiveness strikes me as being of a much earlier time. What do you think?'*

*Pamela looks at me and pauses before responding. 'You mean that she is much younger than she appears.'*

*'Yeah, maybe. What do you think?'*

*Pause.*

*Pamela is beginning to look more confident: 'I think that is very possible. I've got stuck with all this "adult" material but maybe it's not so adult after all. I have to go back with her. Get her out of the mire and confusion of the present and look back towards her time of being young, very young.'*

*There is a palpable sense of relief in the room. We have stopped hating the patient.*

The supervisor has to rely, like the therapist, on feelings that are being gener-ated in the supervision session. Whether the therapist is a counsellor or psychoanalytic psychotherapist is beside the point. When we give attention to the supervisee in the session we have to give it with all our senses, we need to use all our responses to the benefit of the supervisee and her clients.

## Example

*Jeremy, a supervisee with some five or so years of practice, is describing the sexual behaviour of a young male client who, with a friend, following final university exams, went 'on the spree'. They drank a lot of beer and ended up going first to a lap-dancing bar and then to a brothel. This behav-iour was uncharacteristic of them and in retrospect Jeremy's client seemed ashamed of himself. As Jeremy told the story to me it was very evident to me that he felt disgusted at what he saw as sexually demeaning behaviour by his client. He was beginning to pathologize the behaviour of this young client through his own feelings of moral repugnance.*

*I thought the task here as supervisor was to acknowledge the feelings that Jeremy was clearly expressing and to help him sort out what was really neurotic or psychically disturbing material and what was probably no more than a lapse in standards of social and sexual behaviour by a drunken young man.*

*At a later stage we discussed the feelings of disgust that can arise in any of us when confronting sexual practices that we find alienating and which challenge our sexual anxieties and moral codes.*

The example given above leads not only to the possibility of greater understanding between the supervisee and the client but also to a strengthening of the relationship between supervisee and supervisor. So the relational aspect of the session is strengthened by the presence of a technique of working, which sits within it with comfort and intelligence. As I have argued earlier, there is much to be gained by not separating technique from the relationship of the supervision alliance. It is salutary when the supervisor shares the confusion and resistance of the supervisee and is able to use it in a learning process.

A key element of psychotherapy and counselling is to understand the feelings and experience of the client – in the case of supervision, the presented client. In the instances quoted there is present an element of interpretation, which is initiated by the supervisor and taken up by the supervisee. Although it is possible to see interpretation as being, in the possession of psychoanalysis, a product of Freud's theories of therapy, it must be stressed that interpretation is not in possession of any school of psychoanalysis, no matter how distinguished. I would suggest to sceptical counsellors, quite the contrary. We all interpret our sense experiences all the time in our daily lives. The interpretation given in the example of Pamela came to me through a feeling that I began to associate, inside myself, with my experience as a father watching my discontented, tired and upset toddler child going from one toy to another, finding nothing satisfying and collapsing in angry tears. This was my memory. Recalling this experience helped me understand my present feelings about the patient and enabled me to make a hesitant interpretation of what Pamela and I were experiencing in the supervision session.

Interpretation has become something of a shibboleth, a term embraced and held up as special, of value and exclusive to psychoanalysis. The truth is that, if counsellors in particular give themselves the space to think about the ordinariness of the term, they will quickly see that it is in their possession too, to be used as another technique in the therapeutic relationship either in supervision or therapy. The counsellor will not find herself 'telling' the clients what they are experiencing. The better technique is to invite the client to explore for themselves the possible unconscious implications of their thoughts, feelings and actions. Going back to the restless unhappy image of the toddler, which I recall so vividly, it would not be at all unusual to recall a mother saying, as an interpretation: 'He's tired. What he really wants is a kiss and a cuddle.'

It is salutary to remember how often toddlers, offered that interpretation, will resist it, insisting that they are not tired, wriggling protestingly from their mother's arms on the way to bed.

I am not suggesting that the task of interpretation can just be understood as common sense, but rather that it is a way of relating, in the supervision situation, towards both the presented client and the supervisee herself, which requires the supervisor to be alert and questioning in her appraisal of the surface presentation. What I am asserting is that as humans we are constantly calling this awareness into being in our everyday relationships, sometimes unconsciously, sometimes consciously.

Any reading of Freud, especially in his early published works, demonstrates the way he used his awareness to add another dimension to the therapeutic dialogue. Most clients and patients, as they become accustomed to the special nature of the therapeutic/counselling relationship, quickly come to understand the nature of interpretation when it is sensitively applied. The critics of Freudian interpretation who speak vociferously against the notion of the patient/client being told the meaning of their own behaviour by a psychoanalyst are perfectly correct to do so. To tell clients what they really mean by any specific act or statement is a waste of time – bad practice. The task of the therapist/counsellor is to enable the client to discover meaning for themselves. This applies equally to the supervision relationship. Self-discovery has an energy and impact that no amount of telling can hope to achieve. It is truly a learning experience.

As I write this I am becoming aware that much of what is being described and discussed is held within some of the tasks described by Michael Carroll (1995) and listed at the beginning of this chapter. He refers to the relationship task, the teaching/learning task, the counselling task, and these aspects of the supervision role are implicit within the descriptions I have offered above. My position is that all these tasks are embedded first and foremost in the supervision relationship. The boundaries between these tasks are always blurred and fluid as the discussion flows through the supervision session. Tasks should not be isolated and taught as a didactic process structured and ordered in a particular fashion, but rather incorporated into the supervision relationship as a dynamic activity of point and counterpoint, like a dance: the relational approach.

## Time

One of the more objective features of the supervision process, and a task for the supervisor, is the management of time. The management of time appears to be entirely objective, although it should be borne in mind that it was we humans who invented clocks and, in a sense, 'invented' time. Time is a central concern in counselling and psychotherapy and the subject occupies an entire chapter in my earlier publication (Feasey, 1999); it is equally important in the supervision relationship. The regular allocation of time to supervision is regarded by most practitioners as a necessity, especially as we enter the field of counselling and therapy in an active, participatory way. Although the trainee time has passed and with it the most close and scrutinizing aspect of supervision, a new vista opens up where supervision takes on a completely different flavour. It is reconstructed as an equal professional relationship, and time has to be found to provide for it. Time is about frequency as well. In my private practice it is usual for supervisees to meet with me on a monthly basis and this seems to be the norm, although it could easily be challenged.

In certain institutional situations I have seen supervisees more frequently, but in my private practice the demand has not been for intervals shorter than a month. The monthly meeting lasts an hour and a half. Again, this appears to be the product of precedence rather than principle. These practices are all constructs of habit and what has gone before, and I do not suggest them here as being substantial, except in the sense that I am suggesting that, if supervision is to be meaningful, it must have sufficient time and frequency in the calendar of the supervisee and supervisor alike.

There is an expression: 'time is of the essence of the contract', which is a useful one to employ if you are engaging a builder to put an extension on to your house. It simply means that if the contract is accepted then the time specified is binding on both parties. In the culture of counselling and psychotherapy there is little need for such an expression, but, on the other hand, we need to recognize the professional discipline that accompanies the relationship of supervisor and supervisee. It is obvious, from my experience, that on the whole supervisees do keep their side of the contract. On the other hand, I have heard distressing tales of supervisors who have not been so diligent in their role. It is one thing to say that you are going to be available every month at a certain time but it is another thing to keep to the promise against competing demands from clinical clients, interesting conferences/ seminars, professional invitations and, of course, the claims of a personal life. Here I am referring to the supervisor, but I might as well be describing the life of the counsellor/therapist. If we are claiming to be professional in our practice as supervisors, it is essential that we honour the obligations of time without discrimination.

The other aspect of time is how it is used in the supervisory meeting. Personally, I like to use five minutes or so at the beginning of the session to exchange greetings and put my client at ease. This might include offering tea or coffee. The intention is to establish a feeling of meeting as colleagues, essentially equal and sharing in our work as psychotherapists and counsellors. The next use of time is to set up the framework of the meeting. What is going to be presented? We can then think of how much time we need to accomplish the task in hand. From then on I assume the responsibility of managing the supervision time actively, that is ensuring the presented clients are given the share of time we have decided upon, reminding myself and the supervisee of the passing of time as the session proceeds.

This all sounds orderly and nicely controlled, but sometimes the reality is different and the experiential aspect of the supervision session begins to take over and ten minutes has flashed by like a second and we are still only approaching the world of the client under discussion. In such a situation the responsibility of the time management still rests with the supervisor, who has to decide with the supervisee what is to be done. So the situation is dynamic and this is comparable with the counselling/therapy session. The relationship between the two participants has to accommodate and recognize this and respond appropriately.

We all know that time is one of the most elusive of creatures to control. We 'act out' through our use of time. In other words we use time to demonstrate our feelings and memories in an active way and the world of supervision is particularly susceptible to this phenomenon.

## Example

*A supervision group some years ago. The group met monthly for two and a half hours at my house in Manchester. There were three members plus myself. Mostly, members were very respectful of the boundaries of time and our need to get together promptly and sort out, at the beginning of the session, the order of our work as a group.*

*But Jerry was late. He had been late for three sessions in a row, arriving about twenty minutes after we had started and, as a consequence, undermined our order of work, i.e. who should present first, second and third. He rang my door bell. I guessed it was him, put the session on hold, answered the door and let him in. He then went straight to my lavatory. I returned to the room. Silence. We waited. A few minutes later he entered, murmured an apology and took the empty chair. Suddenly, we were thrown into a new situation; our orderly decisions were undermined and questioned by the arrival of this member who had not had any part in reaching the decisions we had taken. What should we have done?*

*My resolution of this occasion was to draw attention to the situation we were now in and insist that we respect the order of presentation while at the same time doing a quick calculation of the time left and how it could now be reasonably distributed. This was accepted, but a friction was present that was to break out into an open quarrel at a later session.*

This is an example drawn from group supervision, and I shall write at greater length about this in a later chapter when discussing group process.

**Memory**

The supervisor has a special responsibility to act as a memory in the supervision relationship. I do not mean the supervisee has no part in this process but that, as with the therapeutic/counselling relationship, the therapist holds the material of her client in her memory, where it is safe and secure, to be drawn upon at the right moment and used to the benefit of the therapeutic relationship, so the supervision session creates a similar situation. As time goes by and a rich history of supervision has been established then the memory of the supervisor is useful for looking back at precedence and relating it to the present concern.

One of the most amazing aspects of the counselling/therapist role is the ability that quickly develops in the therapist/counsellor to remember the client's material. Obviously, sometimes we fail. Sometimes the failure is pathological, and this comes to the supervision session as an important failure. It becomes supervision work focussed upon the therapist rather than the client, other than in the fact that the client is part of the therapist's forgetting.

None of this should unduly disturb the experienced counsellor/therapist, but for newcomers to the business of therapy this forgetting can be very disturbing and may indeed produce deep feelings of shame. There may follow a reluctance to confess to the supervisor the nature of the situation that has come about. Where the supervisor is available as a vulnerable human being to the supervisee, I do not see this as an impossible impasse, but, if the supervisor has set herself up as a didactic authority, a correcting, punishing figure, it is more than likely that the supervisee will hold back and censor as a protective measure. We are all human. Memory is fallible. Indeed, it is often argued that we construct our memories of the past from current experiential material.

Therapists quickly learn to accept that a memory recalled in therapy and transmitted to the supervision session has to be cautiously accepted and sometimes understood in terms that are more of the present than the past. The supervisor has to remember that a memory of a client retold by the supervisee from an earlier therapy session is going through yet another filtering process where quite serious, albeit subtle, changes can take place. We should remember what every experienced police officer knows, that witness statements based on memories are always suspect. No two people report the same incident in the same way.

Thus we have memory in supervision that is multidimensional in character:

1. the reported memories of the presented client/patient
2. the memories of the supervisee
3. the memory of the supervisor.

In all respects it is obvious that memory is a deeply subjective activity, sometimes accurate, objective and dependable as a clear account of events that have happened, sometimes vague and subjective, especially when recalling the true nature of feelings. Most of us can recall recounting an event to a friend where so-called strong feelings have been described only to realize that in the telling these feelings have moderated and changed. So were they so strong in the first place? Or, conversely, there can be the denial of feelings in the telling of the incident. It is common for workers carrying out grossly distasteful tasks, which arouse feelings of anxiety or disgust, to rationalize these feelings through black humour or dismissal of significance. The aim is to reduce the force of the memory and to place it where it will not intrude into consciousness in a disturbing manner.

The complexity of the process of recall and recounting is known to all of us, and Zinkin (1995) reminds us quite properly that much of it is shared fantasy, Not to be dismissed but acknowledged and worked with in the supervision relationship.

## Monitoring

Much of what I am describing under the title of time and memory can be attributed to the process of monitoring as listed by Carroll (1995). Monitoring is not only the notion of remembering but also inevitably carries the suggestion of judgement and evaluation. Going back to my earlier mention of Imre Szecsody's article (1990), we are again encountering the notion of roles in supervision. He emphasizes the idea of a crowd in the supervision room, and I agree with this conceptualization (Feasey, 1996), only adding that other figures can easily enter or leave the room creating a complex of interactions that need to be recognized and taken into account from time to time. Sometimes these figures come and go fleetingly and bewilderingly, which adds to the complexity of the situation.

## Example

*Gill, a mature and very experienced therapist, who I thought I knew very well, began to reminisce about her early days as a young woman in a big northern city. A woman in her late sixties, she was relating a colourful and demanding existence as a twenty-year-old, struggling to live alone and be independent in a large anonymous city, where she knew very few people. She continued to talk of this period of her life and the marriage that she had made and how that had transformed her life. She had gone from penury to relative riches when she got married. Suddenly I realized that the husband she was describing in such glowing terms was not her husband of the present time. I was amazed. Her feelings were so strong and warm. The husband of some forty years ago was with us in the room.*

An interesting sideline to this experience was her tacit assumption that I knew about this first husband. I didn't. But she felt secure in the relationship with me and assumed I was party to this rarely referred to event in her eventful life. As far as monitoring was concerned this experience alerted me to become aware of an aspect of the supervisee's life that could be very influential, especially in the situation of transference and countertransference experiences in the therapy situation and the supervision relationship with me.

Monitoring, in the sense of observing and consciously recording 'progress', in the evaluative sense of the word, is more likely to be present as a strong influence in the supervision when the supervisee is in training. Obviously, the supervisor is watching the work of the supervisee with great interest, watching a potential therapist/counsellor emerge and grow in confidence. The supervisor works to that end, positively and supportively. In my view it is essential that monitoring has this character. There is a great difference between maintaining a watchful position as a supervisor, when that position is imbued with positive qualities, than watching to 'catch someone out' in error with a view to correction.

Monitoring as a concept may act as a prophylactic. By careful monitoring in the supervision situation the supervisor can sometimes anticipate a problem arising that can be dealt with before it becomes influential in the supervisee's work with her client.

### Example

*As a young, in experience terms, therapist I was to likely to fall back on silence when I felt unable to respond appropriately to a client. I hid behind a curtain of therapeutic distance. I would be quite proud of my ability to maintain a silence in either my individual or group work and saw it as a sign of therapeutic strength. Fortunately, my supervisor at the time became aware of my use of silence and began to challenge it in the work I was then currently doing, especially with a private group that I was conducting. At first I was resistant to his enquiries and penetrating observations, but gradually I began to realize the aspect of the way that I was using silence as a defence against the admission to myself of a certain inadequacy. This was especially palpable when I took into account the way I had been shocked when an earlier group I had been conducting simply collapsed as members left, one after the other. A salutary experience!*

Sometimes it takes a painful experience like this in the professional life of the counsellor or therapist to bring us face to face with personal limitations in our work. The sensitive, aware and competent supervisor can help us to confront such failure, if that is what it is, and deal with it in a positive way. Creative monitoring by the supervisor helps to put the work of the therapist/counsellor in perspective, allowing for a personal evaluation by the supervisee that is ultimately positive and reinforcing, rather than undermining.

The story is the same if the supervisor is available as a colleague, a concerned human being, then this monitoring, although sometimes painful, allows the relationship to survive and grow to the benefit of the supervisee and, most importantly, her clients/patients. After all, it is to this group that the task of supervision is addressed in the first and last instance.

# Chapter 9
# Group supervision in private practice

In this chapter I shall be looking at the practice and principles of running a small supervision group from the point of view of the supervisor and examining some of the issues that arise when the supervisor brings the world of small-group supervision to another supervisor. No, there are not too many 'supervisors' in the last sentence!

The BACP noted the special character of small-group supervision in its statement on supervision (BACP Information Sheet no. 8). It identifies two forms of supervision in the group: 'Group supervision with an identified supervisor' and, as an alternative, 'Peer group supervision'. In the first, as is stated, there is an identifiable supervisor who takes responsibility for the work of the group and settles the amount of time and attention each supervisee in the group will receive, or mediates with the group through a process of group discussion as to how the time is best used. It is likely that in such a situation the supervisor will be paid a professional supervision fee, but not inevitably so.

The second approach described in their information sheet is 'Peer group supervision'. It is stated that three or more counsellors share the responsibility for providing each other's supervision within the group context. There would be no designated supervisor present. Normally, the counsellors would consider themselves as of relatively equal status in terms of training and experience. The information sheet goes on to describe some of the limiting conditions surrounding such an arrangement. I have never been in such a group, and I am hesitant about drawing any conclusions about the practice of working with colleagues in supervision without a professional supervisor present, and so I shall content myself by simply saying that I would regard such a setting as possible, but hazardous, certainly not one that I would personally choose, unless nothing else was available.

I have had experience of working as a paid supervisor for a group and supervising a counsellor running a supervision group. I feel confident in my experience to comment on both. In addition to this experience I have, too, a long-established practice in group psychotherapy and group learning in experiential groups, where I have employed theories and practice from the Foulkesian Group Analytic and Yalom (1975) models, but not exclusively so. I was very influenced by the work of Brown (1950) in my early days of working with groups. He seemed to favour an interactive and systems view of group behaviour within work settings. A supervisor working with a group of counsellors or psychotherapists will soon come to recognize that the group rapidly develops a peculiar and special profile of its own – a way of being together – in effect, a group culture that needs to be taken into account as work proceeds.

Coming from a group orientation, I have naturally emphasized such a posture in working with small-group supervisees. But there are other approaches that have become popular in recent times. Bringing creative, quasi-dramatic processes into the supervision group is often seen as a stimulating and agreeable way of working in a novel way, breaking free from the 'discussion' format of most supervision groups (Inskipp, 1996). On the other hand, Colin Feltham (1999, p. 18) expresses reservations about injecting what he calls 'colourful imagery' into the group supervision session, wondering if it leads to 'durably better practice'. I am sceptical of the view that we can easily make these measurements, drawing immediate associations between the method of supervision and specific outcomes in therapy and counselling.

Angela Webb (1999) in her interesting chapter 'The Difficulty of Speaking' considers it likely that there may well be more difficulty for the supervisee in disclosing feelings about her client in a group setting than in individual supervision. It seems to me it is inevitable that within the group process there has to be a period of growth of trust before open admission of weakness or difficulty can be frankly explored in front of peers within the group. On the other hand, experienced group conductors know that as trust builds and peers become accustomed to helping one another in dealing with painful issues the individual becomes more secure and courageous in her work within the group. As individuals progress in the group the rest of the group benefits and the process becomes incorporated into the group culture as a form of mutual help and support. In effect the more experienced members of a group act as a model for newcomers and those who are initially nervous of self-exposure. In time the revelation of 'mistakes' and uncertainties becomes a part of the group culture and safe.

Angela Webb finishes her discussion by coming down heavily in favour of individual as against group supervision, but I think she is being rather pessimistic and not taking into account the expertise that is available to the supervisor from the considerable knowledge of group analysis, which would support the productive activity of group supervision. In the end it seems to me that the supervision is only as good as the supervisor and supervisee together come to make it in and through their relationship with each other. If the group supervisor is knowledgeable about group behaviour and able to utilize the energy and support of the group towards healthy supervision behaviour, it is likely there will be good outcomes for all concerned. Thus she and I will have to differ.

On the other hand, I would willingly concede that, if a supervisee feels inhibited and frustrated in a supervision group over a significant period of time, she would be wise to seek an alternative arrangement. As Barnes, Ernst and Hyde (1999, p. 175) remark, there is a need to attend to the task in hand. If an individual finds the group persistently nonfacilitating, the advice must be to go elsewhere, rather than explore the dynamics of the group for a solution.

Sue Kaberry, already referred to earlier in this book discussing abuse in supervision, gives some consideration to the issue of group supervision in her chapter (2000, pp. 47–49). In her survey she found evidence of counsellor supervisees who had experienced real difficulty in the group situation, sometimes feeling scapegoated or left out and marginalized by the group interaction. Obviously, this can and does happen but a comparative study would probably show the incidence of this kind of experience is no more likely in a group than in individual supervision. A bad supervisor in either context would produce similar responses in those unfortunate enough to be within her control and influence. Kaberry's sample of abused supervisees was a small but nevertheless telling one. She found that not much work had been done in researching this field, and as a result it is difficult to generalize in any way about the current situation. However, she discovered enough abuse in the group situation to make us wary and on our guard when recommending group supervision to others.

My own view is that if the group supervision is based upon a relational approach by the supervisor and she works from the first principle of equality and respect for her supervisees, then the participants are unlikely to suffer abuse. But of course we are all human and a supervisor may be quite unaware of an abusive attitude that she might strike up from time to time. In such a situation it can only be hoped that the supervisees concerned would not be afraid to speak up for themselves.

It should not be forgotten that sometimes supervisors have to grapple with quite difficult minor neurotic responses in the group they are working with.

## Example

*John's supervision group was well established. On the whole he knew his supervisees from relationships outside the group, in the training situation. John had been a senior trainer for some years and was well known. This, however, was a private group, which he had recruited by recommendation and word of mouth. He came to me on a monthly basis for supervision for both this group and some individual clients he was working with in a counselling relationship, with a psychodynamic approach. Thus I was supervising his 'whole practice'. I had a high regard for him as a practitioner supervisor and trainer, but it was obvious, from time to time, that he had to struggle with boundaries and role confusion.*

*Mary was a particularly difficult member of the supervision group. She had known John as a tutor in the training course she had followed and admired and respected him. He had given her a good deal of attention preparing her final year dissertation, and she had become increasingly attached to him throughout this time. Now she was quite rivalrous for his attention from other group members. She would sometimes make her feelings known to the discomfort of the other group members, who would react competitively towards her. So this former relationship, bordering on personal friendship, set up a difficult dynamic to work with inside the supervision group. It had to be addressed in supervision.*

The above situation does not seem to me exceptional in any way. This is another example of experiencing a 'dual relationship', which is bound to occur from time to time. It is probably best to anticipate difficulty arising in such an arrangement, and act in advance to prevent it. Personally, as a supervisor, I would not accept anyone into my group who had been 'in therapy' with me at another time, perhaps as part of a training experience.

Barnes, Ernst and Hyde (1999, p. 175) make an interesting point referring to Zinkin (1995). They argue, in sympathy with Zinkin, that in some respects supervision is an 'impossible profession':

> ...since the supervisor cannot be present at the group session and so does not know what happens, yet psychologically (from the supervisee's point of view) is present. It may work best if both remain aware that what they are jointly imagining is a shared fantasy rather than the truth.

It is clear that group supervision is going to throw up these extra- and intra-group tensions from time to time, and therefore it should be noted that some training in group leadership should be a natural prerequisite to the task of becoming a group supervisor. It then follows that, if the supervisor of a supervisor is working with the group, among her qualifications there should be a working knowledge of group dynamics. This may all sound like 'fleas on the back of fleas', but in the example I have given above it becomes obvious that, for both of us, in that given situation an understanding of groups and their processes was necessary.

However, I am not arguing that all of us need to be fully trained group psycho-analysts. Although it could be assumed that an analytic approach is necessary to be effective in the situation described, my view is that most senior counsellors have had a rich group experience in their training as counsellors and should be able to draw upon that experience to be effective as group supervisors.

For supervisors wishing to extend their knowledge and skills, it should be remembered that some parts of the British Isles can now offer at least a one-year introductory training course in group analysis, which informs at a serious and sophisticated level of training without taking the trainee, necessarily, to further qualifying years to become a recognized group analyst.

Such a group will take the participants into the basic experience of analysing group behaviour.

1.  It will lead the trainees to understand that there are a number of surfaces of behaviour in groups, some of which are very obviously conscious and relatively easily observed and some of which are immediately below consciousness, held there as a protective mechanism. They are often experienced as group, rather than individual, responses within the matrix of the group (Barnes, Herst and Hyde, 1999, pp. 122–123).
2.  It will help the trainee witness and value the place of emotions in the group and the way in which these emotions may be displayed, used and responded to in the group.
3.  It will show the manner of group leadership that encourages the formation of a healthy therapeutic group culture, which abandons a position of 'strength' for 'vulnerability', in the service of the well-being of its membership. Jeremy Holmes (1999) states quite clearly in his foreword to *An Introduction to Group Work*:

    There is an irony in this: the more a group is able to face its weaknesses, the stronger it becomes; the more it can admit to fears and failures, the less likely failure is to occur.

4.  It will lead to an understanding of what is meant by group culture and the way this culture affects the way the group works or fails to work.
5.  It will demonstrate the way in which, although an individual may appear to be the prime source of an anxiety or confusion, the truth may be that this person is actually carrying the feelings for many other members of the group.
6.  It will show the way in which fantasy surrounds the person of the group leader and the imagined power of this role and its influence upon group members (Bion, 1961).

7. It illustrates the manner in which a supervision topic, drawn from the experience of a client by a supervisee, will sometimes begin to actively replicate itself in the life of the group.

These are only a few of the learning experiences that may be gained in a group analytic process, but they are invaluable tools in the hands of a supervisor running a supervision group for psychotherapists and counsellors.

From this training and perspective I was able to help John deal with the potential splits in his supervision group, where there was a danger of his former tutee becoming isolated, attacked by some influential members of the group as a jealous response to her claims upon her relationship with him. I had an experience in a supervision group not unlike his.

## Example

*In one experience of running a supervision group I was to notice and engage with issues of transference, where there was a good deal of intra-group bidding for the greater part of my attention by the individual members. It was thought that I had the final say in the disposal of time, and such was the strength of feeling coming towards me that there was a spin-off of competitive activity within the group. Sometimes this would display itself by members interrupting each other in the supervision dialogue. These were fairly obvious attempts to 'take over' the group's attention with my apparent complicity. On other occasions, as a response to my 'special' position in the group, a member would attempt to displace me when I was commenting upon some material provided by the group.*

I quote this experience to illustrate the way in which a reasonable awareness of group dynamics assists the supervisor in the recognition and understanding of some of the meaning of the behaviour of a group in its work as a supervision group. In the example given above I had to find means of restoring the equality of the group members without entering into a blatant competitive struggle with a member attempting to displace me as the group supervisor.

An importance difference in the position of the conductor of an analytic group, as against the role of group supervisor, is in the style and openness of the latter as against the former. In the analytic group the conductor is likely for the most part to withhold any direct comment of opinion or provision of information, mostly returning such material to the group to deal with. The group supervisor works on a much more open and level relationship, colleague to colleagues, and will undoubtedly contribute to discussion and debate in the group. In my view this does not prevent the presence of transference material appearing, which may be used meaningfully by the supervisor in an appropriate way.

The problem, if it exists at all, is to find a means of identifying the transference presence. Clearly, where a group analyst is less disclosing, it is easier for her to draw attention to transference material. The disclosing group supervisor may have more trouble in identifying the transference feelings and more difficulty in helping the supervisees to recognize and understand its presence and significance. Therapists, in the supervisee role, who have been exclusively trained in a person-centred context may especially have difficulty with locating or accepting the force of influence of the feelings I am describing.

Having described a certain kind of problem in group supervision it is probably useful to look at some of the obvious advantages in group supervision.

1. The presence of other supervisees sharing problems and achievements in the supervision group can be very reassuring to individual members . It is all too frequent that therapists find themselves very isolated with doubts and anxieties. The presence of others facing the same or similar dilemmas is reassuring.

2. A group can produce a rich potential of experience from which the members may draw. A difficulty expressed and described by a supervisee may well have been in the professional history of another member of the group, who can empathize and offer commentaries that prove useful. Often such a contribution supports the supervisor and substantiates her reflections.

3. Group solidarity tends to hold individuals who need to contemplate and examine very painful failures or confusions in their practice as counsellors and therapists 'safely'.

4. A group provides an opportunity for the supervisor to marshal support for and assistance to a member who is floundering and losing confidence, or is threatened with severe disturbance by outside influences.

### Example

*William, an Asian supervisee in a supervision group, was being threatened with disciplinary action by the head teacher of a special school, who disapproved of his methods of work with some highly disturbed, autistic early adolescent boys and girls. William had a multidisciplinary role in the school. He was employed both as a teacher and a child psychotherapist, and sometimes the boundaries between these two roles became very blurred. In supervision he confessed to the clash of role culture and explained the ways of working that he adopted to lessen any pathological outcomes. He set up a group of teachers and their assistants meeting once a week in a lunch time to explore the dilemmas that many of them shared. It began to look as if the head teacher, who was not therapeutically trained, was feeling threatened by his initiative.*

*William's reaction to this situation was a mixture of defiance, anger and anxiety. He was an intensely creative person, and his work with the children reflected his creative insights and skills. He found it almost impossible to tolerate any interference with his values and creative feelings and thoughts in his work with the children. The fact that this was coming from the head teacher, who was also the proprietor of the school, made the situation even more difficult for him.*

Working with William in this situation, I was glad to be able to call upon the support of the other members of the supervision group, all creative therapists, who had a natural professional sense of identification with him. Together we were able to disentangle what was reasonable in the head teacher's complaints, based as they were on her unfamiliarity with the approach William was using, giving rise to anxiety in her to which she was responding in a repressive manner. We also engaged with his anger, which threatened to overflow into his relationship with the head teacher with possibly disastrous consequences.

5. A supervision group is in itself a training situation for the participants, who become aware of the processes of the group and the manner in which they may be helpful or impeding in the work of supervision. It provides an education in human communication.

Although it appears that the learning will be primarily concentrated on group experience, it is inevitable that the participants will acquire psychological skills and insights that will offer them general support in their work as therapists and counsellors in whatever context they are working.

However, a word of warning from Barnes, Ernst and Hyde (1999, pp. 175) who, in discussing the supervision of group therapists in a group setting, write:

> This means that supervision groups are complex and both supervisor and supervisee need to think about how best to use them. Both can be seduced away from the task in hand into preoccupation with the group setting, with the individual supervisee's blind spots or the dynamics of the supervision group itself.

6. On a practical level the supervisor of a private supervision group will often feel she is making good use of time, especially if the supervisees come to her chosen place of supervision. In addition, the fees paid by the group members represent a good source of income. My own practice

with the group I was running was to allow two hours for the group, bearing in mind that it had a membership of three. This allowed time for each member of the group to work and some time for a cup of tea with a short exchange of social greetings and gossip. Each member of the group paid me £15. That was some time ago, and now I would ask for an individual contribution of £20. We established a contract concerning fees, attendance and notice of leaving or closure and the introduction of new members, which was done with group consent after full consultation. All meetings were held at my home, where I have a consulting room.

In my experience these represent the main positive features of supervision in the group.

These are some disadvantages that are apparent and were experienced in my own group supervision situation.

1. **Transference**. The relationship between supervisor and supervisees is less intense and less obvious, attention to it may not be focussed with sufficient energy and concern. Similarly, a supervisor may fail to recognize her own transference feelings, whether of warmth or coldness, towards a particular supervisee, with distorting outcomes. It is as well to remember that not all feelings of warmth or coolness arise from transference. There are 'real' feelings in a group that arise from firmly established features of the reality of the personal relationships.

2. **Individuation**. An individual may experience the group as marginalizing and excluding at a time when she wants undivided attention from the supervisor. This is not necessarily a neurotic response by an individual; it may simply reflect the problem of drawing attention to oneself when there are a number of competing siblings, some of whom may actually be frustrating your attempt to gain attention.

3. **Splitting**. The group might attempt to keep the supervisor on the margins of the group and deal with the supervision activity in a possessive, controlling and excluding manner. This is a very complex and threatening activity as far as the healthy life of the group is concerned. It may not survive this attack.

4. **Resistance**. The group might 'waste time' in all kinds of ways, including socializing at the expense of the work time, resenting attempts by the supervisor to get them to address the reason for being together as a supervision group.

5. **Rivalry**. The group might split into a rivalrous two-against-one scenario in an attempt to exclude a member and to have the supervisor to themselves. Not at all an uncommon event.

6. **Narcissism**. Sometimes it is difficult for the supervisor to allocate time and attention equally when the neurotic demands of individuals predominate in the life of the group. There is always the danger of one member becoming isolated and thus alienated as the supervisor struggles to maintain an equilibrium of time and attention in the group.

7. **Boundaries**. Late coming, early leaving and failing to give advance notice of non-attendance can be very distracting and undermining to the work of the group and usually has pathological meaning.

8. **Conductor**. The supervisor has an extra responsibility and task, as group conductor, which might distract from her performance as a supervisor in the first instance. Barnes, Ernst and Hyde (1999) draw attention to this problem. Combining the two roles of conductor and supervisor is sometimes difficult and beyond the capabilities of the supervisor.

9. **Anxiety**. If personal relations become tainted in the group, frank and open revelation of difficulties become more difficult to expose. Censorship becomes present in the group, which distorts the work and presents a great problem to the supervisor in her work. (This situation is representative of what Angela Webb (1999) warns about. It is discussed earlier in this chapter and needs to be taken seriously.)

10.**Practicality**. Practical problems arise in arranging suitable times and dates that will suit everyone in the group, offering scope for 'acting out' by individuals in the group. Foulkes (1948, p. 168) wrote about the recapitulation of early family experience by individuals in the group and sometimes this conflict and failure to agree within a group is symptomatic of such early family experience.

All these experiences occurred in the supervision group I was running. We dealt with them as a group, as they arose, often at my instigation. Sometimes it was difficult and painful to address the issues, but in the long term they were resolved to a degree of satisfaction and, in my view, they provided a learning situation for all of us.

So the balance of pros and cons is pretty equal, but do not in my view invalidate group supervision as a valid way of working. It can be very rewarding.

In closing this chapter I would like to remind readers that this is a description of the possibilities and drawbacks experienced in a privately run group. The situation was of my own creation and I had the ultimate say in the life of the group. There was no external force or authority to constrain, inhibit or decide the construction of the group. And, finally, there was no assessment of performance in the group beyond the privately held views of the individual members. For me this is the big attraction of working privately, and I remember the years of bureaucratic and professional struggle in NHS mental hospitals with some amazement. I am surprised I survived as well as I did.

The greatest strength in the supervisor is the quality of her experience in becoming a counsellor or psychotherapist, of whatever discipline. The basic principles of the training and practice remain the same in the process of running a supervision group. As counsellors and therapists, we are encouraged to put the needs of clients first, even when they are once removed in the supervision situation. After the well-being of the primary client comes the need of the secondary client, the supervisee, who will hold a priority position in our concern as supervisors. The usual codes of confidentiality and non-disclosure will apply and be respected by the supervisor, even if not by some members of the group. Boundaries will be made clear and respected by the supervisor, as an example to the rest of the group, and a contract supporting 'good practice' will be agreed between the supervisor and the group, both individually and as a group. This is the very basis of a relational supervision group.

All this is routine in the procedure of psychotherapy and counselling. It is this essential 'conservatism', in practice, that provides the security necessary to a productive situation. Defences can be safely challenged and properly addressed, where the relationship between supervisor and the group is open, genuine (in the Rogerian sense of this word), uncensored and evenly balanced in terms of power and influence, remembering the supervisor is there to learn as well as the supervisees.

# Chapter 10
# Group supervision in institutional settings

In this chapter I continue to look at the practice of group supervision but now draw upon my experience of working in two large hospitals, where I was for a time responsible for supervision with NHS professionals, some of them experienced in psychotherapy and counselling and some of them not. I also did some teaching with junior doctors.

It is well to remember that forms of supervision existed in the medical culture of hospitals long before the practice of either individual or group psychotherapy became present in any significant way. Virtually all medical personnel, from whatever discipline, in their practical training receive supervision from their mentors, senior figures in their profession. The work of the supervision is primarily tutorial; it is concerned with the manner of learning by the supervisee, with a heavy emphasis upon procedures as well as clinical knowledge. Goldie (1986) vividly describes his experience in an NHS general hospital, as a psychotherapist attempting to bring a psychoanalytic view to bear upon certain presented clinical symptoms that had not responded to formal examination. The response of the medical staff was at first entirely sceptical.

The supervisees are placed inevitably in an unequal relationship to the supervisor, even though the personal professional relationship may be friendly and supportive. Indeed, my experience of teaching junior doctors showed me, plainly enough, the admiration and loyalty they often felt for their consultant and the strong bonds of loyalty that existed between them. They were like members of close families, supporting and defending themselves behind closed ranks of mutual identification. At the same time the hierarchical structure of the supervision was obvious and accepted as inevitable by the clinicians concerned.

Although the history of counselling and therapy supervision is very different, it too can demonstrate this hierarchical structure in certain instances. I would be the last to maintain that psychotherapy supervision is always different from the more traditional medical forms. I have noticed that doctors and senior clinical psychology staff working in psychotherapy, with a strong background and training in traditional formal approaches, sometimes find it hard to abandon this experience when dealing with junior staff. There has to be a real effort of will to embrace the culture of counselling and psychotherapy supervision.

There is a strong element in the practice of supervision with counsellors and therapists that emphasizes quite a different stance on the part of supervisor and supervisee. The stance is not medical in its form. The emphasis is placed upon a more equal relationship, a place of mutual learning and essential respect for the value of the supervisee. The responses between supervisor and supervisee are not so much based on the correctness or incorrectness of therapeutic procedures, but rather on the meaning of the supervisee's work with the client in the dialogue of the therapeutic situation. That meaning is brought into the supervision as a shared vision upon which the whole group, including the supervisor, will reflect.

The supervisor does share with the medical supervisor an overarching responsibility for the well-being of the presented patient/client, which is expressed towards the client/patient being presented in supervision. This is a value shared, without reservation, between the different professions. Ultimately, the well-being of the client/patient must come first. However, it is no simple task identifying the nature of 'well-being'. It is not an activity or concept in the sole possession of the therapists concerned. On the contrary, the strongest voice in the process of discovery must lie with the presented client/patient.

Another very large difference between the supervision in medical professions in the hospital setting and the psychotherapy supervision setting is that the medical setting for the supervisees will almost certainly be homogeneous. Such discrete supervision groups, representing different professions, would be in a rivalrous situation with each other in the hospital setting. Their disciplines would jealously guard their professional training and special competencies, against the claim of other professionals in the hospital. The tasks would of necessity contain large elements of defensive material and forms to protect the clinical performer. By the time young professionals come to work in a hospital, they have assimilated this idea of 'task' and its accompanying form and content. If they are challenged, tensions arise, and the task performer, nurse, psychologist, doctor, occupational therapist or whoever will experience a challenging tension (De Board, 1978).

These tensions were very evident to me twenty years ago when I first went to work sessionally in a large mental hospital as a psychotherapist. In my view they are still present to this day and constitute a real problem to NHS reformers, who come from outside the system and do not appreciate the powerful nature of the defences that are quite naturally employed by special clinical interest groups within the institutional structure. This needs to be borne in mind, remembering that twenty years ago there were no counsellors or analytic psychotherapists present within either of the hospitals I worked in.

Lewin (1952) explored the subject of field theory and its relationship to institutions within social science and discovered the presence of powerful rivalrous experiences felt by practitioners. Supervisors coming to the task of working dynamically with distinct clinical supervision groups, each of whom has a particular history of training and practice, must take into account Lewin's and de Board's findings concerned with defence against anxiety, which is a primary need in any clinical group of professional therapists dealing with human suffering and distress.

However, in the heterogeneous psychotherapy supervision group the aim, jointly shared and respected, was the good practice of psychoanalytic psychotherapy, and the group was mutually supportive in this task. The usual rivalries and tensions of usual practice and seniority were abandoned, albeit with difficulty, in favour of learning together and working with the supervisor, in this case myself. It is quite common for a psychotherapy supervision group to be heterogeneous. I can recall a supervision group with a clinical psychologist, mental health nurses, a social worker and occupational therapist present. The presence of the psychologist was especially remarkable at the time in question, when clinical psychology was completely dominated by behavioural therapy training, but his presence and contributions from a strong discipline of psychological training proved exceptionally useful to the group.

The nurses present had to abandon the traditional distance that they normally occupied in relation to patients; they had to abandon their uniform, the social worker had to give up her 'authority' and the occupational therapist his preoccupation with therapeutic 'occupations' of a social and objective character. There was no doctor present, but, if there had been, she too would have had to abandon the traditional authority of drugs and medication to work at an equal 'level' with those normally subordinate to her decisions.

It is to the credit of psychotherapy supervision that it challenges the demarcation lines that separate the professions. The presence of this influence is most largely represented in situations where the institution creates special therapeutic communities that operate on dynamic lines, where all the staff, irrespective of professional identity, are required to work with patients psychotherapeutically in a dynamic mode. Although such communities are not all that common, their influence has been powerful and the presence of multidisciplinary psychotherapeutic teams is generally accepted. The other place where such teams work together is in day units for psychiatric patients who, living in the community, still require therapeutic support and treatment.

These teams are invariably multidisciplinary and often incorporate a culture of cross-disciplinary work; so, for instance, a nurse or doctor may work in a creative therapy setting alongside a drama therapist or art therapist, or a clinical psychologist may share the responsibility of assessment with an occupational therapist, social worker and charge nurse. This pattern is then reflected in supervision groups. I think one of the big influences at work lies in the fact that most advanced psychotherapy training occurs at a post-professional training level. The culture of psychotherapy education emphasizes equality and encourages a mix of disciplines and the presence of lay people such as myself in training groups.

Kennard (1998) discusses the question of supervision in therapeutic communities in a way that offers guidance to those working in the day-centre setting. He distinguishes between that kind of supervision that is essentially task-orientated and that which is mainly concerned with community relationships. He weighs up the opportunities of supervision coming from inside the membership of the community staff, stressing how helpful it is if the supervisor has a good grasp of the 'way the community operates'. He does recognize the difficulty that may arise, too, where the supervisor may be someone who is 'blinkered by his commitment to seeing the community in a particular way' or is a recognized authority figure. This, too, may distort the role of supervisor in the eyes of other staff members.

My own view is that in such a situation it is better if the supervisor comes from outside the staff team and is not identified with any particular staff member. The disadvantage (Kennard, 1998) may be that the supervisor, coming from outside the institution, may not be well enough informed about the way the therapeutic community works – its special practices and rituals – and therefore is likely to 'miss' important aspects of work that need to be addressed in supervision. My own view is that, though this is a possible handicap in the early stages of supervision, the sensitive supervisor will soon come to understand the way things are done in the community, with its team of therapists and patient community.

For some years I worked as an outside facilitator to a clinical psychologist service staff group, based at a large mental hospital. At first I found many of the references made by the team to the life of the clinical psychology department, especially in its relationship to the larger hospital setting, difficult to follow and fully understand, but I soon learned the meaning of this language and could gauge its significance to the psychologist staff group.

Although clinical psychologists still maintain a high professional profile in hospitals, it is of some significance that in recent years they have been readily accepting counsellors into their staff teams, in a manner that would have been seen as improbable only a few years ago. These counsellors will also meet with their psychology colleagues for supervision. More commonly, counsellors are being employed in GP practices, working alongside doctors, practice nurses and sometimes social workers. Here there is a greater problem for the provision of appropriate supervision.

At this point I would like to acknowledge the existence of Balint Groups. These are experiential groups set up by general practitioners in which they meet as peers to discuss the confusion, the pain and problems they experience in the work with their patients. It has something of the nature of a therapy group and a collateral peer supervision group. A fuller account can be read about the nature of these groups in Christopher Dowrick's article (1996).

Balint Groups are exceptional, the exception rather than the rule. In most GP practices the situation seems to be more complex and the dominance of the medical model appears to be almost absolute. The leadership of the medical practice by a 'senior partner' seems to be critical to the culture of the practice as a whole. This stems to some extent from the fact that most of these practices are modelled on private businesses where the doctors are partners and the rest of the team are employees. Counsellors in particular are likely to experience difficulty in finding appropriate supervision in this situation.

**Example**

*Robin was an experienced, well-trained counsellor, who had done advanced training in group analysis; he was a sophisticated supervisor and trainer. The need to earn a living took Robin into work with a large GP practice. The pay was not good, and there was no supporting contract. Getting any increase in sessional fees seemed to rely upon getting the ear of the senior partner in the practice and, in this case, the doctor concerned (a woman) was most elusive. She seemed to sense the purpose of Robin's approaches and fended him off with her justifiable 'busyness'. The result was frustration and anger in Robin, which he brought to supervision.*

*Together we worked out a position for him to adopt, and we took a close look at his approaches, which were invariably on the spur of the moment and fed into the frantic work culture of the practice. We also looked at his larger position as a counsellor of advanced training and experience, in an attempt to make an evaluation that would help him increase his self-esteem, recognize his own worth and increase his earning power.*

I do not think his position was that exceptional. More recently a counsellor friend who works alongside a clinical psychology team complained ruefully of being the worst-paid member of the team and saw no way of addressing the issue with his psychologist colleagues. It may well be asked whether this is the concern of supervisors. My view is that it is. It falls into the category that I have described as being involved in the supervision of the 'whole practice' of a supervisee. In this case the underlying issue was of professional 'value', which is, more often than not, measured in terms of salary. The emphasis for the supervisor is upon standing for the 'good' treatment of the presented client and that must remain as the priority of the supervisor, but in doing this it also remains an imperative to look to the well-being of the supervisee, in whatever aspect of her professional life she is struggling with.

Although the issue of payment in the instance given above may not be the main or sole concern of the supervisor, the position of the supervisor in her care for the supervisee is, in my view, central to the supervision relationship. In the instance quoted it is probable that the issue of money is enmeshed with feelings of lack of self-esteem and a sense of being inferior in the situation described. In this instance the supervisee becomes the presented 'client'.

There can be no absolute ruling in this interpretation of the range of the responsibilities of the supervisor or what is or is not of concern to her in the supervision dialogue. Everyone taking on the role will in due course find issues, beyond the immediate concerns of patients and clients, requiring a professional response.

I have been emphasising the responsibility of the supervisor towards the patient/client as occupying a powerful place in the supervisor's concern, insisting that this is a truism, applied wherever counselling and therapy supervision takes place, whether with an individual or in groups. Keeping discussion focussed and pertinent to the needs of the therapeutic relationship is an imperative. Recently, I was interested to read a fascinating article in *Changes* (1988) on this question, particularly on the mode of the analytic group and its ideology (Sharpe, 1995). This is especially true, too, for people in group supervision where the material under discussion will be worked on by three or four people as well as the supervisor and the presenting supervisee.

It needs to be borne in mind that, although it is true that the supervisor is 'present' in the therapy/counselling encounter, the presence has a fantasy character about it that will certainly impact on the counsellor's/therapist's performance, but not in any objective sense as the supervisor. The supervisee is especially aware of his own vulnerability and likelihood of making 'mistakes', which he shares with other trainees. This is particularly true in group supervision.

There have been attempts to 'objectivize' the supervision of group psychotherapy by having television cameras in place to record the therapy session; this is then scrutinized by the supervision group. Aveline and Dryden (1988, p. 323) describe in some detail the technical requirements of such a situation, where the positioning of camera, microphones and the presence of technical support staff are imperative concerns. Frankly, I feel it is very unlikely that most NHS workers would have access to such sophisticated technical support. But, even if such a position becomes possible, there are both ethical and psychological reasons for treating this proposal with great caution.

The presence of a camera and microphones acts as a particular kind of psychological stimulus to group behaviour. Although people sometimes claim that they soon got used to the camera and 'forgot' about its presence, the reality is that, at an unconscious level, the camera is remembered and responded towards. Technology is not neutral, even though many people like to think it is. The person controlling the camera occupies a position of immense power in the process of choosing the shots: close-ups, medium shots and long shots. The choices are inevitably governed by deeply subject-ive concerns. A person is shown shaking her foot: is this a more important piece of non-verbal communication than someone staring at the floor? Who makes this judgement? What will be recorded? Who decides?

As a former professional TV presenter I am often very surprised by the naïvety of many psychotherapists when they engage with programme makers, professional or amateur. Often ethical issues become blurred in favour of the values of the media. A recent television broadcast of a therapeutic encounter within a very highly valued institution raised anxiety in me, which was not supported by many of my psychotherapy or counselling colleagues. So one anxiety was added to another! Or was I merely being mildly neurotic in my concern for the ethics of the situation? The whole basic provision of confiden-tiality had been abandoned in the programme concerned, although there were and are perfectly sensible techniques available to programme makers for maintaining confidentiality if they choose to do so.

One of the most obvious ethical concerns is in respect of the fate of the recorded television programme or audio tape. Who controls its use and movement within an organization is a vital issue. The subjects of the recording very rarely have any say in the disposal of tapes. In my experience these issues seem not to impinge upon the consciousness of psychotherap-ists and counsellors as sharply as they might do. It appears that our age of mass communication is dulling our ethical sensibilities.

I worked in a clinical psychology team where a determined young psychologist took control of therapy session/supervision videotapes and insisted that they:

a) never left the department, no matter what the pretext
b) were deleted immediately after the supervision/therapy session had finished.

She took this determined and rather unpopular stand after discovering staff had been taking the tapes out of the department without thinking through the ethics involved in their actions. They were naïve rather than wicked! I was much relieved at her intervention and backed her up on every occasion I could.

It is difficult to answer the question of what the reality of supervision really is. Where does reality begin and end, and what constitutes the reality of the practice of supervision?

A sophisticated, psychoanalytic view of group supervision is not very often met with or understood in institutional settings, where the experience has been that supervision is concerned with objective, proper and 'true' clinical procedures. For these values to be reset into the context of shared fantasy in a group is not an idea that is immediately welcome or appreciated where the institutional tradition is markedly different. Describing his journey towards becoming a professional counsellor, Robin Rigg (1998) reflects:

> Supervision was mentioned as being – as a general source of support and ideas – a way for new counsellors to be less worried about making mistakes, because *somebody else knows what is happening and is ultimately responsible* [my emphasis].

In reality this is bound to strike the experienced reader as a somewhat naïve view of the role of the supervisor. It is as well to remember that, as Zinkin (1995) argues, much of the material discussed in supervision is of a fantasy-like character. Memories of the therapeutic encounter are rather as a result of distorted memory, defensive distortions and elaborations arising from the therapeutic relationship. In no sense is it to be regarded as literally true. Zinkin, having been an analytic-group psychotherapist, would obviously have been influenced by the idea of the controlling presence of the unconscious and its influence on the process of perception in all human beings, especially in psychotherapy settings. But this concern is not necessarily shared by other mental health professionals, as is illustrated by the following example.

### Example

*Gill worked in a psychiatric day unit. She was an experienced psychotherapist coming from a creative background of therapeutic training in drama therapy as well as psychotherapy, she was multiqualified psychotherapist and accepted as such by a professional institute and her counsellor/therapist colleagues. She was required to attend group supervision on a fortnightly basis with her day-unit colleagues, most of whom were nurses and occupational therapists. The senior charge nurse 'ran' the supervision session and regarded it as a chance to review the patients attending the unit, which she did on the basis of date of entry to the unit. No other aspects of the life of the community were addressed.*

*The charge nurse regarded it as within her province to decide what was material for the group and what was not. When Gill tried to bring in issues that were concerned with patient transference experiences in the unit and countertransferences expressed by the staff, the charge nurse failed to recognize its significance or countenance the presence of the material in the supervision group. She openly suggested that the concerns expressed by Gill were 'highfalutin', essentially theoretical, and had no place in the supervision group. She was angrily uneasy and dismissive. Gill also became increasing angry and frustrated in the group and brought her feelings to the individual supervision session with me, thus we were faced with institutional limitations that were virtually impossible to address within her workplace setting.*

I am not suggesting that all group supervision in NHS settings are so 'token' and misapplied as in this example. But my experience was that often 'approved' procedures imposed from above would be reinterpreted when put into practice by workers who were not, in the first place, sympathetic to the practice required of them. Sometimes this reaction was defensive simply because the necessary retraining of clinical workers had not been implemented when reform procedures were implemented. In such circumstances it is not surprising that the reforms become merely 'token gestures'.

In my experience, the procedure that suffered most from this syndrome was the creation of counselling groups in day units where the group leaders, usually nurses, were sometimes completely untrained in respect of that procedure. For some time, with the co-operation of other colleagues, I attempted to run intensive courses for nurses who were placed in the unenviable position of running groups without proper training or the presence of good professional supervision. The costs of the training to the participants were small. Unfortunately, at that time 'in-service training' funds were rapidly drying up as far as clinical workers were concerned, and the bulk of training money appeared to be going into management training and 'higher' levels of training for more advanced clinicians. So my efforts were frustrated.

I would stress that these comments are based on my particular experience in a particular NHS area and should not be interpreted as applying to services over the whole country.

Whatever the frequency of this occurrence, it represents a very real challenge to any supervisor confronted with such a situation within an organization where the norms of group supervision are not clearly understood. Often the supervisor has a 'political' role in educating the organization in such a manner as to change and enhance the existing supervision arrangements that are in place. My own view is that an 'outside' supervisor has a better chance of bringing about change than someone from within the organization. I find as an independent practitioner I can sometimes insist upon certain organizational reforms when I am negotiating a supervision contract.

In my experience I think counsellors are less likely to experience the discomfort of having to work dynamically in a potentially hostile supervision situation that is hostile to the language and propositions of psychotherapy. This is partly because the counselling ideology, where unconscious processes are not given great weight, is not so threatening to psychologists and medical clinicians, who place emphasis upon the paramount importance of immediately observable phenomena. This is not to suggest that they won't encounter difficulties. Far from it. Issues of their status and authority seem to emerge when they work in institutional settings, whether in GP practices, hospital and day-care units or clinical psychology departments. All of these units will have some arrangements for the supervision of their clinical staff and the supervision may take any form or have any emphasis, depending upon the culture of the unit concerned. This may or may not meet the needs of counsellors, who usually have little power to change the arrangements.

It is apparent that, because of the longer standing of psychoanalytic psychotherapy generally and its influence among certain distinguished consultant psychiatrists, the status of the psychotherapists from this background is more assured. Certainly, when I went to work in an NHS day community centre as a psychoanalytic psychotherapist some fifteen years ago, this was reflected in my sessional payments and in the fact that I was 'managed' administratively by the top-grade clinical psychologist for the local mental health services authority. Although he was entirely behavioural and cognitive in orientation, he was always most supportive. I was recognized, too, without difficulty, by the Department of Health in London. To some extent my status and position in the hospital reflected this institutional support coming from London.

My supervision was handled by a consultant psychiatrist with a special interest in psychotherapy. With this level of support I felt reasonably secure. The resistance to my presence came from the nursing staff, occupational therapists, some of my colleagues in the clinical psychology department and the conventionally qualified psychiatrists. I think a counsellor might have had a much more difficult time in establishing her autonomy and standing in the NHS at that time. Certainly, there would have been very few people in post who could offer sensitive and supportive supervision.

For a supervisor from a therapeutic or counselling tradition working in the NHS within an institutional structure there could be real problems of communication as expectations concerning her role become confused. This would include the confusion of medical staf who, being trained in a very different tradition, might be not only puzzled by the supervisor's observation but actually alienated by them. The supervisor, too, may experience difficulties, especially if she finds the basic assumptions of some of her supervisees reflect a different value system to her own.

Although not drawn from a hospital setting, the following example illustrates problems that arise when a therapy culture is in conflict not from outside interference but from unrecognized internal tensions.

### Example

*Jim was working as a supervisor with a university counselling service for students. He had been invited to take on this responsibility and was adequately paid for his fortnightly services. He took up the appointment enthusiastically, although he was well aware of the severe time limitations and framework of restricted provision that university counselling services invariably apply. He worked in a group with some very experienced counsellors, and this included the leader of the counselling team. There was a parallel group, which he did not meet, and which was supervized by another person.*

*From the beginning Jim experienced difficulty as a supervisor as he struggled to come to terms with the short-term interventions of the counsellors. Most students received about six sessions of counselling. Often their presenting problems were symptomatic of deep-seated problems, usually arising from dysfunctional family relationships, which to their surprise followed them to university, where, of course, they hoped to escape them. The counsellors, all well trained and experienced, recognized this dilemma but were persuaded by the conditions of their employment to opt for short-term interventional counselling, rather than long-term, interpretative, relational therapy.*

*The situation remained like this for about a year. Jim grew more and more concerned with his position in the supervision process, feeling compromised with the arrangement he had to work within. But at the same time he enjoyed the contact with an intelligent and rewarding group of counsellors, one of whom had been trained in a psychodynamic tradition and another of whom was clearly responsive to some of his interpretative supervisory remarks.*

*The resolution came at the end of the year when a review of arrangements was called for. The leader of the team had become involved in an important and committed way with the newly emerging form of therapy called 'cognitive analytic therapy' and was anxious to promote it within his service. So Jim's contract was not renewed, rather to his relief, although he knew he would miss the contact with the counsellors towards whom he had developed warm professional feelings.*

This example simply illustrates the muddle that can follow when even an experienced supervisor such as Jim takes up an offer that should be refused.

The implications are manifold. It appears that supervisors need to be aware that supervision is not just a technique of working with counsellors and therapists. The supervisor has to recognize the dissonance that can arise when there is a clash of training and practice philosophies. The most obvious problem shown in the example given is the inherent differences that apply when short-term, as against long-term, counselling is provided. The time of the short-term work is limited by negotiated agreement with the client, and the long-term work will probably continue, open ended, until either the client or therapist/counsellor calls a halt. This means that the procedures of therapy and counselling are markedly different in each case and sometimes stand in contrast to one another. If the supervisor of a group of counsellors or therapists finds herself seriously uneasy with either approach, she would be well advised to think again before taking on the responsibility of supervision.

It has to be recognized that counselling and therapies of all kinds have their specific philosophies of practice, which contain ethical and value assumptions that react to any challenge. Merely to describe supervision as a method of assisting clients and therapists is misleading. The reality is that the supervisor becomes deeply associated with the working philosophy, moral and ethical assumptions and therapeutic approach of the supervisee. This can be either a comfortable or uncomfortable experience. Whichever applies, it is up to the supervisor in the relationship with the supervisee to address the issues concerned.

Angela Webb (1999) explores the research in this area and bears out this view. Webb not surprisingly affirms that the interpersonal relationship of supervisee and supervisee is critical to the accomplishment of good work in supervision. The more trust, the better. Where the element of trust is compromised, the work in supervision is flawed.

Before concluding this chapter I wish to touch briefly on the matter of supervision and its application to group-analytic groups. It is a specialist subject in its own right and group analysts have their own literature of reflection and description, which they refer to in training when seeking to understand the place of supervision in the process of group analysis (Foulkes, Bott, Zinkin, Pines, Sharpe, and Hyde, Barnes & Ernst). I intend to make only a few references to material that might interest the reader coming from a different perspective, and in doing so hope not to offend group analysts with its necessary superficiality.

At the beginning of this chapter I pointed out that group supervision, in this context, was meant to apply to heterogeneous groups. I regard homogeneous groups of therapists as coming into quite a different category of concern. Interestingly, Proctor (2000) in describing the typography of super-vision groups simply assumes that all the counsellors come from the same basic counselling culture. I think this is debatable.

Supervision in groups for group analysts is part of the inherent training mode of group analysts. Foulkes (1975) believed that the centre of group-analytic training was occupied by the process of supervision. Supervision in the group culture of group analysis is complicated. The issue for many super-visors in such a role is how much they take notice of and use the unconscious processes of the supervision group, Barnes, Ernst and Hyde (1999, p. 175) suggest that both the supervisor and supervisee may be:

> seduced away from the task in hand into a preoccupation with the group setting, with the supervisee's blind spots, or the dynamics of the supervision group itself .

For the most part, supervision groups in hospital and other similar institu-tional settings will not consist of a majority or exclusive group of group analysts (Bott, 1979). On the contrary, there might be one such skilled profes-sional group worker present who has to work alongside therapists from a variety of training and practice. On the other hand, in certain specialist units there may well be sufficient group analysts to form a homogeneous supervi-sion group. When this occurs, the problems set out by Barnes, Ernst and Hyde may apply. It does occur to me, however, to consider the problem further. My own assertion of the value of relational supervision might well take into account the psychological processes of the group and certainly the supervisees' 'blind spots'. After all, what is the 'task in hand'? to quote the authors again. It seems to imply a falling back into the position of supervision as a discrete method, with its own and separate agenda of concern. This seems to me untenable in practice. The demands of the supervisees for a deeper and more 'therapeutic' approach are evident to anyone who regularly conducts supervision with psychotherapists and counsellors.

My view is supported somewhat by a short but interesting chapter by Bryce W. MacLennan (1966) on the subject of training. He writes:

> One very interesting type of experience we have noticed in supervisory groups is the re-creation of the climate or problem which is being described in relation to the therapy group. In this situation the therapist [*supervisee*] seems to play the part of the patient or group of patients.

H. H. Wolff (1966) in the same publication discusses the same experience and suggests that it seems possible to work within the didactic mode and the therapeutic mode, reconciling their presence alongside one another.

Proctor (2000, pp. 106–107) pays some attention to the issue of the dynamics of supervision groups and shares my view that sometimes the internal intra-group relationships have to be addressed by the supervisor at the expense of the attention normally given to the presented client/group drawn from outside the group. So it is possible for the dynamics of the supervision group to become *the task in hand*.

This phenomenon is, I suggest, quite common in the individual supervision situation, and so it does not surprise me that it occurs in the group situation. Of course, it raises questions about the nature of supervision and at one point it shades into therapy. Personally, I do not regard this as a fearful phenomenon. Sometimes the obvious thing to do, if the supervisee is currently 'in therapy', is to suggest she takes the problem to her therapist. But often this is not the case. When this is so, I do not think one should brush it aside or ignore it in favour of the supposed *task in hand*. This is the essence of what I have described as the relational approach.

**Example**

*A very experienced and mature woman therapist, Anna, whom I see regularly for supervision, works within a difficult mental hospital situation as an analytical psychotherapist. She sometimes says, as an introduction to the supervision session: 'Well, this isn't strictly speaking supervision material; it could be thought of as stuff for my therapist, if I had one!' She then goes on to outline anxieties about the working situation that she wants to discuss and understand better in the supervision dialogue. She may even be experiencing a 'blind spot' in her relationships with other therapeutic staff, not an altogether rare or unusual situation. She might be talking about a feeling of stupidity or distance that comes over her when she realizes that today is the day when Mr Brown comes for therapy and the relief she feels when it turns out that Mr Brown has rung in sick and cancelled his appointment. Whatever the issue, I feel the supervisor, in this case myself, has little option other than to work with the client, in this case Anna.*

To conclude, it is obvious that supervision in institutional settings, whether in the somewhat rarefied atmosphere of the training institute, or the down-to-earth day centre in the High Street, presents problems and challenges to supervisors working with the therapists concerned and, through them, their clients.

This chapter merely explores some of the issues. The resolving of the issues can take place only in the particular settings in which they occur. No formula for dealing with them exists outside the context of their occurrence. So supervisors, supervisees: *be prepared.*

# Chapter 11
# Supervision in the creative therapies of dramatherapy and psychodrama

A statement from the British Association of Dramatherapists:

> Supervision is necessary for effective dramatherapy practice. All qualified dramatherapists, having taken out FULL MEMBERSHIP of the BAD, are required to undertake forty sessions of clinical supervision within the first three years following completion of their postgraduate diploma course. In addition supervision is recommended for all dramatherapists throughout their working lives.

As yet the British Psychodrama Association has not made a formal statement concerning supervision.

However, I am aware that all psychodrama trainees are supervised in training by their designated and recognized trainers within the BPA. It is an inherent part of their training. My view is that as more psychodramatists emerge from training, the practice of seeking supervision by these therapists will stimulate and provide a supervision service.

Some readers may wonder why I have included a special chapter on these two therapies and where its sits with the rest of the book. My answer is partly personal and partly professional. I was for many years qualified/skilled in dramatherapy, psychodrama and psychoanalytic psychotherapy, and I tried all the time to draw these disciplines together in my work as a therapist and inside the professional bodies to which I then belonged. This was sometimes very difficult. The various therapies present in the mental health services are sometimes rivalrous to one another and sometimes very slow to recognize the worth and presence of new therapies entering the NHS. In my lifetime as a professional therapist I have seen dramatherapy and psychodrama develop from very small tentative beginnings into well-rounded, sophisticated and effective psychotherapies, now increasingly present and influential in the NHS and private practice. I have considered myself fortunate to have played a small part in this development.

Hence the presence of this chapter in this book. The other reason for its presence is because I have been privileged to be a supervisor for both dramatherapist and psychodramatist psychotherapists, and I wish to include this experience in this text for the benefit of readers across the disciplines of therapy. The intention is to draw the practice of supervision of these creative therapies closer to the practice of supervision in psychotherapy and counselling. The chapter does not intend to claim to train or inform existing supervisors of creative therapists, many of whom are very sophisticated practitioners, rather it is intended to draw traditional psychotherapists and counsellors into a closer relationship with their colleagues in creative dramatherapies. Indeed, it is not uncommon for non-dramatherapists working as psychotherapists, especially within the NHS and Social Services, to supervise colleagues who are dramatherapists or psychodramatists. Sometimes that is a happy, collaborative experience, sometimes not.

In addition, I am not going to write about or consider the particular problems of music- and art-therapy therapists, who have special features of their own that are beyond my competence.

In an interesting research survey carried out by Madeline Andersen Warren and Lorraine Fox in 1999 they identified no fewer than eighteen different work settings for dramatherapists, 176 of whom responded to a total of 240 sent questionnaires. It was deduced from this sample that no fewer than fifty-five people worked in multiple settings, the biggest single group; thirty-two people worked for a single organization and twenty-eight worked as freelancers.

It is quite likely that the fifty-five who worked in organizations would have experienced, over a period of employment, various models of supervision. These supervision models might well have related to the wide variety of therapy interventions practised by the dramatherapists. Dramatherapists provide a therapy service for many forms of psychological disorders, and physical and intellectual impairments. It is clear from the research that a large number of the sample were being supervised by therapists from other disciplines from a very broad band psychotherapies. In the research quoted here it is quite clear that the dramatherapists concerned stated as a first preference a desire for supervision from another dramatherapist, as against a therapist from another discipline. It is with this evidence in mind that I have written this chapter, confirming as it does the need for supervisors, from whatever background and initial training, to bring the special needs of creative therapists to bear upon their perspective when offering supervision.

Perhaps the first thing that has to be established in the dialogue with practitioners of dramatherapy and psychodrama is that they are, by training, talent and tradition, associated with the live theatre, its culture, forms and its history. This background is often remote from their co-therapist colleagues in the NHS, who might regard the supposed glamour of the theatre and acting as far away from the serious business of psychotherapy and counselling. My own journey from some early experience of acting and directing to psychotherapy was a long and far from consistent one. This is not a biography; so I will spare the reader much further revelation. However it was on this path I first experienced what was described in the 1950s as 'creative drama', 'educational drama' or, sometimes, 'remedial drama'.

This form of drama was mostly devised by talented and exceptional drama teachers such as Jim Burton (1955), Peter Clough, Alan Garrard (1957), Brian Way (1967), David Clegg (1965), S. C. Evernden and Peter Slade (1954) and used with children. There was one particular exception, Robert Newton (1937), who, when working with depressed, alienated unemployed miners in Wales in the 1930s, saw the possibilities of using 'free drama' to expand and develop the lives of the men with whom he was working. What was meant by 'free' drama was simply that it was not bound by text. The material for drama was created by the participants themselves and worked into dramatic form through improvisation and the help of a experienced director. Usually, the dramatic material reflected the lives of the performers. This was the basis of his approach to working with the miners, and it became a productive, creative success, which inspired him to build on its success and others to follow in his wake.

This approach is so common now that most people would regard it as unexceptional and accept its validity without much question or comment. But in Newton's time it was novel and challenging. There was an 'establishment' of those in the world of theatre and drama who opposed such experiment and thought it a dangerous challenge to the traditional 'literature' of the theatre and the work of the playwright. Indeed, it is probably true to say the amateur actors and producers were particularly hostile to this approach, whereas some professional actors and directors had themselves been experimenting with new theatre forms and showed more sympathy and understanding. In our own time the work of renowned film and theatre directors Mike Leigh and Peter Brooke stands as a testament to the validity of this form of dramatic invention.

As far as the use of drama in therapy was concerned, during the rise of this creative drama movement in education, it hardly registered as a possibility in the world of mental health medicine. There may have been one or two bold nurses or occupational therapists at the time who saw the possibilities and experimented with creative drama as a therapy, if so they are unknown to me. It was not until Sue Jennings appeared on the scene with her book *Remedial Drama* (1981) that drama as a therapy began to be taken seriously and the Association of Dramatherapy was born. Not long afterwards Marcia Karp came to this country from America where she had trained and became an experienced and capable psychodramatist from the Moreno school. A rapid development in training psychodramatists came about as a result of her presence in the UK and the Psychodrama Association came into being.

Dramatherapy, an essentially British creation, can trace its roots back to this early movement in creative drama, and numbers of dramatherapists, like myself, had experience in formal theatre acting and production as well as 'free drama' on our road to becoming dramatherapists.

Thus, long before dramatherapy established its presence, there had developed a strong 'creative drama' movement working with children of all ages where the emphasis was upon improvisatory drama, movement and dance, again free of choreography and devised by the children themselves as a form of self-expression. It was through this movement that I entered more closely the world of 'drama in education' and youth theatre, a movement regarded as promoting the emotional well-being of children and young people. There are too many innovators and teachers to mention here. Many of them took up influential roles in teacher training colleges and university departments. Suffice it to say that this movement became recognized and influential long before dramatherapy became a coherent organized body of thought and action.

Interestingly enough, there was no suggestion or thought of supervision in this creative-drama movement. However, when we began training teachers of educational drama in the 1960s, 'teaching practice' had to be overseen by the trainers to satisfy the regulations concerned with the granting to students of the status of 'qualified teacher'. This was required by the DES and the validating universities. In my case I was 'qualified' by London University after training as a drama teacher at Trent Park College of Music, Art and Drama. Later, when training teachers in Lancashire and leading a degree in drama and education, the validating university for my course, which was specifically in drama and education, was Lancaster. This University provided generous creative support through its board of studies and external examiners, in particular Dr Jim Burton, Evelyn Gibbs, both now deceased, and Dr Mary Bell, now in the USA.

The supervision my department offered trainee teachers was very different from the supervision that is offered clinically to trainee dramatherapists now. The emphasis for the teacher was to comply with the aims of education, the organizational structure and ethos of the school and the needs of the children. Work was always with groups of about thirty children, and there was little room for the meeting of individual needs except within the context of the teaching group.

A supervised teaching practice in drama had very different aims from that of the supervision of the dramatherapist today.

Where does the likeness between 'creative drama' and dramatherapy become evident?

The supervisor of the dramatherapist today has to recognize that this particular therapy, as well as having as its own reference points to the usual psychotherapeutic concerns, has to embrace certain specific skills that are particular to itself derived from its drama/theatre origins.

## Example

*Jennifer was a teacher/dramatherapist working in a special-needs school. It was a private establishment, and Jennifer did not 'get on' especially well with the proprietor, who acted as principal, or with the deputy principal. But she was valued by the management for her theatre skills. It seemed that, while her dramatherapy position was barely supported, her ability to organize and present productions by children was well thought of. This paradox, so obvious to the outside observer and hopefully to the reader of this text, did not impact on the conscious concerns of the directorate of the school with any therapeutic emphasis. For obvious reasons the dramatherapist came into her own at Christmas time or when the school organized open days, which made it necessary to show parents creative work in progress. She was used to promote the school to the parents and the outside world in general, but her therapeutic presence was not encouraged except by some discerning parents, engaging with her through their children.*

It is this blend of dramatic/theatre knowledge and technical skill and the therapeutic position of dramatherapists that makes them so special in the world of therapy. I can think of no other group with this particular quality. Of course, there are dramatherapists who have no experience of production and theatrical acting, and this is increasingly so as the training courses develop. But, nevertheless, some of the basic requirements of theatre remain present in the work of these therapists. The obvious one is the question of a protected space. This may seem so fundamental that it will be taken for granted. But this is not so. It is a basic problem for dramatherapists, especially those working in hospitals and day centres. Another issue that frequently arises is the one of admission to the dramatherapy group. Who decides? One would think it is obvious that the dramatherapist should carry out an assessment and admission procedure, but this is often far from what happens.

## Example

Here I am referring to a case of gross mismanagement within the NHS, which I have already partially described elsewhere.

*Jane worked in a large mental hospital, within a day-centre provision. She was attached to a multidisciplinary team of mental health workers. She was the only dramatherapist and the only worker with psychodynamic training and experience. Her clinical manger was the senior OT within an occupational therapy department. Her line manager was a senior clinical psychologist who worked within a tradition of behavioural therapy. There were many contradictions and problems present. One that emerged over and over again was the issue of admission to and discharge from Jane's specialist dramatherapy group. She was not allowed clinical control over these important decisions and a senior charge nurse, a member of the team, would unilaterally discharge patients from the day centre and consequently from the dramatherapy group without consultation with Jane. Thus her group was distracted and seriously undermined by a system that she could not effectively challenge or control. Neither her line manager nor her clinical manager saw any inconsistency in the situation.*

*Her supervisor had to draw her attention to the way in which inappropriate management was actually harming Jane's patients. It seemed likely that the only way that Jane could resolve the situation for herself was to leave and take up another post, which eventually she did.*

This is an example of the way in which the standing and special skills of a dramatherapist might go unrecognized within an institutional setting. The puzzle is why Jane was appointed to her post in the first place, when clearly there was no understanding of the implications of her work as a therapist. I have found this not to be unusual. Sometimes, in the NHS, there is an atmosphere of improvization and compromise that affects all clinical workers. Frequently it is caused by a lack of resources, sometimes by a basic misunderstanding of the needs of the therapist and counsellor, and sometimes there is a deep rivalry between disciplines, which is hard to address. Jane struggled to accommodate to her situation and managed, against all odds, to do some good work before she left this post. I offered her support as her supervisor.

The situation for psychodramatists can be even more difficult. This stems from the fact that they are trained in a tradition and form of therapy that requires a very specific structure of work. It has its own language, sometimes quite unknown to other therapists, and forms of work exclusive to its own practice. The question of space and privacy is an issue for psychodramatists. In an ideal situation they would require a protected space where they can control all the use of the area and keep their equipment safe and free from misuse. The psychodramatist may wish to create a special acting area lit with theatre lighting. She would probably want a good sound system and a stock of simple props and costumes. Platforms are especially useful to create specific psychodramatic areas of performance.

Psychodrama is a particular form of psychotherapy, which is essentially social in character. Another feature of psychodrama training is its insistence upon the strength of the group as a psychotherapeutic presence. In this respect it is close to group analytic psychotherapy. However, there are very real differences here too. Group analytic therapy approaches therapy, very specifically, with the assumed presence of unconscious influential forces in the group. My experience of most psychodrama training and practice is that it invests primarily in the conscious world of the participants. This is not to say that there is no variation in approach from the one described. Virtually all psychodramatist psychotherapists have quite distinct personal ways of working, invoking their own creativity and view of psychotherapy.

My book (Feasey, 2000) tries to address the issue and bridge it by proposing an awareness of the unconscious in psychodramatic therapy, as does Holmes (1992). But this is a minority view and the greater part of psychodrama is conducted with the assumption of the primacy of conscious feelings. In this respect it does not represent quite such a threat to the orthodox approaches of medicine and nursing or, for that matter, counselling. Its main difficulty is its requirement for a long term of training and special facilities when it is put in place in a therapeutic milieu. As I have already mentioned it should be remembered that, although psychodrama and the teaching of Moreno (1946) has a strong tradition in the USA, with a presence that is fifty years old, it has only arrived to have an effective presence in the UK via Marcia Karp (1991) and the British Psychodrama Association, within the last ten years or so. A contemporary supervisor, working with the psychodramatist psychotherapist, needs to be informed of it as a developing therapy, where new ideas are in the making, and where an energetic dynamic of professional discussion and practice is at work.

At this point I would remind readers that the imaginative features of both dramatherapy and psychodrama, so highly valued by those therapists and employed creatively in their therapies, would probably not have been seen as of any great importance to Freud. Mitchell (1995, p. 25) points out that Freud was somewhat dismissive of the imagination and, indeed, saw it as more of a threat to good mental health rather than an aid. He associated it primarily with the infantile fantasies operating sometimes to the production of neurotic or even psychotic responses in the adult. On the other hand, we know that Freud, on a professional visit to France, was greatly attracted by the hypnotic dramatic work of Charcot, the French neurologist, at his Salpetriere clinic in Paris. He tried, quite unsuccessfully, to emulate the cathartic approach back in Vienna (see Clark, 1982, p. 140).

Regrettably, many psychoanalytic psychotherapists of today seem only to encounter imagination as a feature of fantasy in the memories and dreams of their patients/clients. The most they are likely to do with such fantasies is to ask their clients to freely associate with them through discussion. The notion of the client responding to their fantasies in dream form through action in dramatherapy or psychodrama is remote from their usual training (Feasey, 2000, pp. 139-140). That imagination and creativity are important attributes of humanity and are of great value to the individual and society is often not recognized in mental health services. A great limitation.

This has implications for supervision when the supervisor has been trained in the analytic tradition. Nevertheless, it would be misleading to suggest that no contemporary thinkers in psychoanalysis, therapy and counselling have written appreciatively about the function of imagination and creativity in the process of healthy human psychic growth and development. Three who immediately come to mind are the already mentioned Mitchell (1995) Winnicott (1974) and Rogers (1967). All of them acknowledge the importance of 'creativity' and imaginative communication, which Rogers sometimes associates with 'congruence'. Winnicott identified the significance of the imagination in the creation of 'transitional symbolic objects' that play, in all senses of that word, such a fundamental and critical part in the life of the developing infant and child. Generally, child psychotherapy celebrates the importance of spontaneous playful imagination, working through its manifestation in young patients towards healthy outcomes for the child. And, of course, Moreno urged us to 'stand in the shoes' of the 'other', which is an exercise in playful imagination in itself.

For such psychotherapists and counsellors the links between play, creativity and imagination are understood as essential features of progressive therapy and its enquiries. I would go as far as to say that, when we encounter a child who is unable to play imaginatively and enjoy fantasy, we are disturbed and wonder if all is right with the child.

I was very pleased, while working at the Beckhterev Institute in St Petersburg, Russia, when the director of this large mental hospital, in a conversation with me, placed a great deal of emphasis upon aesthetic therapy. I was surprised and delighted, not expecting such understanding and appreciation of the value of the creative imagination in what was then the USSR. I found that in psychotherapy workshops both clinical psychologists and psychiatrists were eager to work creatively, symbolically and with lively dramatic improvizations through dramatherapy and psychodrama.

The conscious use of fantasy in childhood needs to be seen as 'normal', indeed as an essential developmental feature of childhood and adolescence that lingers through into adulthood. It is often very active in our childhood, although usually hidden from adult gaze and hearing (Feasey, 1972, p. 18). This fantasy activity frequently takes the form of dramatic action in which the child casts herself in all manner of dramatic roles, usually adventurous and heroic or glamorous, or all three!

This use of drama and 'acting' is very common and accepted in childhood as normal. It is obviously a means of trying out various social and emotional positions and enjoying the excitement attached to the roles. We discover ourselves in action, either as inside or as outward performances. It is helpfully transformative.

In both dramatherapy and psychodrama this transformational activity can be used in therapy as a potential healing activity. Jennings (1990, p. 12), perhaps the foremost thinker and innovator in the formation of dramatherapy, insists upon the requirement for human beings to rework their life experiences. Play, drama, ritual, role-play performance are all the same means, she says, of carrying out this essential task. We encounter and enjoy different audiences at different times in our lives.

Given this extended special therapeutic value and action, epitomized by dramatherapy and psychodrama, it should be easily recognized that the supervising therapist would be greatly assisted in having knowledge of its character and implementation. Even if that appreciation is only partly informed, there is an essential need for the supervisor to support its value and efficacy in the psychotherapeutic relationship. If this support and understanding is missing from supervision, the creative therapist is seriously impaired and frustrated in her search for sound clinical and relational support within her profession.

I have been hinting at the problems of supervision for the creative therapist working in psychotherapy. I know that both the British Association of Dramatherapy (BAD) and the British Psychodrama Association (BPA) have for some years been working hard to establish the presence of supervision in the training and practice of their supervisees and therapists. It has represented problems, especially in the early days when qualified and experienced practitioners were thin on the ground and some trainees and newly arrived practitioners had to look to supervisors from other therapeutic disciplines to obtain good supervision. Even today the distribution of dramatherapy and psychodrama specialists is uneven throughout the UK, especially for the latter. A solo worker, from either discipline, working in a geographically remote situation could experience difficulty in finding a professionally qualified supervisor trained in dramatherapy or psychodrama.

So the creative therapist is likely to have to look elsewhere for a supervisor from another training background, either someone from a psychotherapeutic or counselling background. But this is not such an easy alternative as might be assumed. Both dramatherapists and psychodramatists are accustomed to working in an 'active' mode; a way of working with which only therapists from their own background might be familiar. Wharam (1992) writes:

The interaction between internalised roles of therapist, client and supervisor (Jennings 1990) can be a challenging format for group supervisors and merits a three-act play of its own ... sitting down ... and using words to describe interactions and feelings is somewhat alien to dramatherapists and 'action' seems necessary.

This desire for action may not be a primary condition in supervision with creative therapists, but certainly it can be present and needs to be responded to when it occurs. Working with dramatherapists, I have noticed how often some of them need to get to their feet to illustrate a moment from their therapeutic encounter with patient or client. One of the most obvious and effective ways of using movement is to invite supervisees, either in a group or in an individual session, to illustrate their issues through the technique of sculpting. Symbols can be used to illustrate particular psychological or social situations to good effect, often vividly demonstrating the essence of an issue being addressed.

What does seem to be a first condition is to have a supervisor who is competent and experienced in the techniques of the creative therapies. Someone who 'has been there' and has experienced a range of techniques in a therapeutic situation. This provides the supervisor with material from which to respond to the supervisee. The response will, of course, be similar in the work with the supervisee, as it is in all therapeutic supervision situations and my advocacy of the 'relational ' approach applies as much in this situation as it does in the world of counselling and psychotherapy, The assumption in choosing a supervisor is that this person is at the basic level familiar with the special emphasis of your training, and, if there are special skills involved, as there are in dramatherapy and psychodrama, they should, where possible, be present.

**Example**

*A senior dramatherapist with some training in psychodrama, working in an NHS mental hospital, is struggling in supervision to find a way of working effectively in one-to-one mode with patients. I know he is familiar with the psychodramatic idea of a stage, a place where action is portrayed. It occurs to me, too, that he is well aware of the concept of the therapeutic boundary. Thinking like this and talking to him, we slowly begin to conceptualize an approach where the patient arrives and sits in a boundaried* **discussion space** *where ideas can emerge that will be followed through, when mutually agreed upon, within another area: the* **stage**. *Afterwards the patient returns to the discussion space to share the experience at another level with the therapist.*

*He agrees to experiment with the approach. We shall discuss it again in a future supervision session.*

This discussion arises out of our mutual experience of the psychodramatic approach, its structure and action. Although we are in a dramatherapy supervision session, our mutual technical knowledge provides the basis for a fruitful discussion.

It might be argued by some supervisors that this search for a technical solution is not the business of the supervisor and supervisee. I can only disagree. I do not think this type of dialogue threatens the other dialogue that looks to explore the therapeutic relationship between supervisee and patient. Neither is it an exclusive activity. There is an 'instructional' feature in this description of the supervision session. As the supervisor, I was teasing out, with the supervisee, an approach to dramatherapy that I thought would be appropriate to his circumstances. To have withheld this idea would have been merely perverse and certainly a denial of the relational approach to the supervision relationship.

I am arguing that a technical knowledge of the forms of psychodrama and dramatherapy, as well as a genuine appreciation of the therapeutic features of these disciplines, can prove immensely useful in the supervision of creative therapists. This does not, however, exclude the need for the supervisor to be an informed psychotherapist with a wide range of training and knowledge, which can be used fruitfully in exploring relational concerns.

## Creativity

Shakespeare put it well:

*The lunatic, the lover, and the poet,*
*Are of imagination all compact:*
*One sees more devils then vast hell can hold,*
*That is the madman; the lover, all as frantic,*
*Sees Helen's beauty in a brow of Egypt:*
*The poet's eye, in a fine frenzy rolling,*
*Doth glance from heaven to earth, from earth to heaven;*
*And as imagination bodies forth*
*The forms of things unknown, the poet's pen*
*Turns them to shapes, and gives to airy nothing*
*A local habitation and a name.*

A Midsummer Night's Dream, v. i.7

One of the most valued therapeutic aspects of dramatherapy and psychodrama is the presence of 'creativity' in the performance of either of these therapies. A glance at the *Pocket Oxford Dictionary* shows the meaning of the word. It talks of 'bring into existence', 'originate', 'inventive' and 'imaginative'. All these terms are indicators of highly valued human attributes. As well as celebrating these traits in ourselves we look to artists especially to offer these experiences to us, and most people understand, quite intuitively, the necessity of such qualities in their lives. Sometimes it is the very absence of these qualitative experiences in the life of our clients and patients that indicates emotional disorder. In schizophrenia, paradoxically, it is often the chaotic representation of these same attributes that indicates severe mental disorder. Unfortunately, too often the psychiatric response to this manifestation of the disordered imagination is to treat it with a drug therapy, which virtually closes down all the creative capability of the patient. Sometimes, but rarely, there is some attempt to make sense of the disorder represented by the imaginative, highly coloured activity of the patient's mind. When this does occur, the outcome can sometimes be useful to the therapist and therapeutic for the patient.

Either way, the presence of imagination, originality, spontaneity and creativity in the human being is a powerful aspect of being and its balance is of vital importance to the well-being of the human psyche. Most dramatherapists and psychodramatists are people who greatly value the presence of creativity in their own and other people's lives, and it is through this belief and understanding that they have been motivated to become psychotherapists.

It is of importance that a supervisor – working with a therapist attached to this viewpoint – who is exploring creativity as a prime 'curative' feature of the human condition, needs to share and encourage this assumption.

**Example**

*Jane brought some of her work to the supervisory session. It was quite tangible. It took the form of a recording of a radio play that her patients had improvised from their own experience, rehearsing and polishing it so that it could be recorded on audiotape. Jane's expertise with, and possession of, high-quality recording equipment made all this possible. She was, too, a skilful sound recordist able to insert music and sound effects to good effect. The patients were delighted with this work and saw it as a great accomplishment. Their own participation was the essential substance of the drama that the therapist was able to enhance and produce. It was something worth holding in their otherwise difficult and sometimes barren lives. As a supervisor, with a professional background of work in sound and television production, I could appreciate the quality of creative work that Jane had brought to the lives of these patients.*

Although a knowledge of and training in psychoanalytic or person-centred therapy is of great value to the supervisor, the appreciation and acceptance of the creative element of a human being, as a therapeutic resource, is an essential condition of her work, if it too is to be 'creative' and productive. Landy (1992, pp. 97–99) makes a powerful case for emerging therapies and places special emphasis upon 'creativity' as a central feature of their presence. A supervisor, working with creative therapists, would do well to familiarize herself with his remarks.

Marina Jenkyns (1999, p. 186), an established trainer of supervisors in dramatherapy (see Conclusion) emphasizes that 'the trainee does not become a clone of the trainer but is enabled to find her own way of working from the firm base of an initial theoretical framework.'

Here Jenkyns is echoing my own concern with the respect for dramatherapist and psychodramatist supervisees: valuing their training and practice, and recognizing their essential authoritative autonomy.

Central to that theoretical framework is the idea of creativity as a powerful therapeutic form, a framework of personal and group expression. Jenkyns (1999, p. 189) also emphasizes the need for the supervisee to work as a creative manager. The aim is for the therapist to discover authority within herself and her practice as dramatherapist, in order to activate the creative therapy that requires a firm framework. The need is for a boundaried structure of organization in which to work effectively.

Jenkyns also appears to advocate the use of the model form of reflection proposed by Hawkins and Shohet (1989, pp. 65–68) in the training of supervisors programme. These are:

1. reflection on content of the therapy session
2. exploration of strategies and interventions used by the supervisees
3. exploration of the therapy process and relationship
4. focus on the therapist's countertransference
5. focus on the here-and-now process as a mirror or parallel of the there-and-then process
6. focus on the supervisor's countertransference.

There is obviously a good deal of overlap between these titles. I have no objection to thinking about the process of supervision in this way as a means of keeping oneself clear as to the journey to be made in a supervision session. But the danger is that in the hands of a naïve or relatively unskilled supervisor the whole approach could become somewhat mechanistic and discrete in a divisive manner.

A skilled supervisor is required to move with a degree of subtlety between the reflections suggested by Hawkins and Shohet in accordance with the demands of the supervision session. The guide to this movement will rest in the relationship between supervisor and supervisee.

Jenkyn's perspective, which she calls 'psychodynamic', tends towards the contemporary school of Freudian analysis, and my own emphasis, outlined in what I have described as 'the relational approach', is towards interpersonal emphasis in supervision, with the supervisor playing an emotionally emphasized part in the supervision relationship, hence the relational approach as described earlier in this book.

In the end it is up to the supervisor to find an approach that is sympathetic to her context of work and personal disposition.

To conclude, we would be wise to remember that all therapists, of whatever school, are 'in role' (Johnson, 1992) when they perform as psychotherapists and counsellors. We are performing an 'act' that requires us to assume a certain appearance, form and way of being that is the special part of the role. This is equally true for those of us who are supervisors, wherever we come from in our orientation. There is nothing insincere or lacking in genuiness in performing this role; on the contrary, the requirement is to perform the role, embracing the best of human values that we can muster from inside ourselves. When we fail to do this, we flounder; to quote an old dramatherapy proverb:

'A dramatherapist out of role is like a fish out of water' (source unknown).

It should be remembered that a creative dramatherapist and psychodramatist can bring great warmth and satisfaction to the lives of the patients/clients. Not all therapy has to be gloom and doom and pain. On the contrary, good creative therapy can offer opportunities for deeply felt satisfaction and a sense of accomplishment difficult to replicate elsewhere.

Equally, a supervisor who fails to understand the need to perform the role sensitively and responsively, embracing happiness as well as sadness, like a good actor, will flounder too and probably sink altogether.

# Chapter 12
# Training and other questions

The American psychoanalyst Reuben Fine (1992) writes:

> In spite of ... errors ... the careful process of individual supervision, as practised in analysis, is still the most practical method for teaching psychoanalytical technique. It is realised that the therapist [supervisee] is not only engaging in an intellectual exercise about the principles of psychoanalysis, but also resolving his/her analytic superego; the greatest progress is then achieved. In this way, the supervisory experience becomes just as therapeutic an endeavour as the actual analytic process.

This quotation relates directly to psychoanalytic psychotherapy learning, but much of it would apply, using different language, to supervision in counselling and the learning process that occurs in that situation. And it raises the question again about what precisely the process of supervision contains. It also raises issues about the nature of the supervisor in her relationship with the supervisee and how the supervisor should be prepared for this event.

At first sight the notion of training for supervisors seems very attractive. Patricia Grant (1994) advocates the training of supervisors and quotes, in support, Bernard (1994). But, and this is a big but, what kind of training is being advocated? Any form of training carries with it an ideology and value system. Most of the relevant books concentrate on supervision as a series of procedures: when one is mastered and completed, move to the next one. Implicitly, or explicitly, many of them seem aimed towards the trainers of supervisors, providing them with a structure and a didactic framework of logic and thought and procedure, which can then be taught (Holloway and Carroll, 1999).

Another way of looking at the situation is to start with the supervisors – of whom there are a great many – the majority of whom are not trained or in training in any specific supervision system. All of them will have been influenced by their training experience as counsellors and psychotherapists, where they will certainly have experienced supervision themselves.

It seems to be assumed by a number of senior therapists, counsellors and trainers that supervisors do need training. As I write I have perforce been researching and reading a number of substantial books (Holloway and Carroll, Stoltenburg and Delworth) that not only assume that supervisors need formal academic training, but set out quite elaborate curricula that should be followed. These books appear to be aimed at the increasing presence of psychotherapy and counsellor training in the higher-education sector of our society. When training occurs in such settings, whether it be in counselling or psychotherapy, it is inevitable that the culture of educational studies impacts upon such a regime. The outcome is that intellectual, cognitive approaches are favoured by the trainers; they tend to look for procedures of training that can be assessed in ways with which they are familiar. Furthermore, the content and form of training will tend to reflect procedures with which they are familiar. Clearly, some trainers in the academic sector are well aware of this tendency and try to ensure that it does not dominate their training approaches. But it is a problem and needs to be addressed. Similarly, if the training is conducted within a medical/psychiatric setting, similar problems emerge. Medical education is long standing and pervasive in the medical services of the UK, whether in physical or mental medicine. Sometimes it is difficult to remind medical trainers that both psychotherapy and counselling do not derive primarily from a medical model of therapy, although there are connections that may be identified and encouraged.

I have reservations concerning supervision training proposals that spring predominantly from a practice and theory that is not, in the first instance, drawn from the world of counselling and psychotherapy. That is not to say that, when in training, supervisors should pay no heed to learning theory and the advances that have been made in the world of educational studies, which may be sympathetically associated with learning to be a supervisor.

The prime experience in training supervisors should, in my view, be experiential. This implies that theoretical postulates should be discovered through the analysis of practical experience. This experience may well be found in group learning, with the sharing of ideas and practice between professionally mature therapists and counsellors, led by an experienced supervisor familiar with group-learning techniques.

In the present educational climate there has been a regression to ideas of teaching and learning that implies the 'expert' provider and the 'empty' learner and quantifiable, measurable outcomes of what has been taught. It has to be acknowledged that sometimes lectures and seminars in psychoanalytical thinking have followed this rather arid path of teaching and learning. I have sometimes struggled with fatigue and the desire to sleep when a well-meaning lecturer, at a psychoanalytical conference or seminar, has 'gone on and on', leaving no space or time for discussion and the sharing of experience between the audience and the 'top table'.

An earlier theory of learning placed emphasis upon 'discovery' (Piaget, 1955) and the careful opening up of personal experience to the scrutiny of the self and others. Vernon (1971) points out that much learning arises from activity – social and physical. Early learning in particular reflects the importance of this creative activity in the human learning process. In other words, there is an assumption made that the learner has valuable relevant information in her possession, drawn from her intellectual, emotional, physical and social life as a human being. Mostly, learning is accumulated as a spontaneous activity arising from an environmental stimulus. The basis of the learning in an educational context in adulthood is to associate these possessions with new material introduced by the teacher. Such a view sits easily beside what I have described as a relational approach to supervision. It implies a creative, interpersonal relationship between learner and teacher, which is essentially a journey of discovery, explorative and imaginative in its essential assumption of the mutuality of learning.

Trainers of supervisors would be well advised to note a reservation expressed by Stoltenberg and Delworth (1987). They are actually describing the placement of trainee counsellor and therapists, but here their remarks (on page 149) are pertinent and can be applied to supervisor training. They write:

> Some students, at some phases of training, find a good match in settings that are relatively open and unstructured. Others, because of individual characteristics or developmental level, are consistently frustrated and overwhelmed in such settings.

Thus, in prescribing an approach to the training of supervisors, it should be remembered that individual differences between trainees need to be taken into account. The 'discovery' method of learning certainly isn't everyone's 'cup of tea'. For some therapists the road to becoming a supervisor needs to be more formally structured, which will provide a higher degree of security and certainty. A variety of schemes on offer with particular ways of training would be welcome to provide diversity and choice. The real problem that arises is where there is an external validating body, such as the UKCP or the BAC, which *may* try to enforce, or at least encourage, similarity and which frowns upon difference in approaches to learning and teaching. The effect of such enforcement can be stifling.

I realize that as yet I have not answered the question put at the beginning of this chapter. Do supervisors need to be trained? I suppose the answer could be 'Yo': Yes and No. It can be asserted that the very process of becoming a counsellor or psychotherapist is a process of personal discovery and learning, and this is then amplified in the actual practice of counselling and therapy. This experience is the bedrock of good supervision practice and is a necessary precursor to working actively as a supervisor. So has this process 'qualified' me as a supervisor ? I think it has, but some may argue it has not. However, as things stand at the moment it will be only a minority of supervisors who have received formal training specifically in the practice of supervision.

Asserting that I feel competent as a supervisor demands some examination of what processes are necessary in the experience of becoming a psychotherapist or counsellor. I would suggest the following aspects of experience and learning are the minimum requirements in the spiral of learning that the would-be supervisor needs to have explored.

I first came across the concept of the spiral level of learning many years ago when I was reading some Jungian literature. I was most impressed with the notion of learning experiences moving through different levels of awareness as we develop as human beings. Spiralling from one level of awareness to another, according to our level of increased development, sensitivity and our willingness to confront new meanings, is a deeply satisfying activity. This seems to me part and parcel of being a client, therapist and supervisor. The following are some positive suggestions towards identifying the spiral of learning that occurs in psychotherapy, counselling and supervision.

1. The experience of paying close attention to the communication of the client at a number of levels at the same time. Thus there is the conscious, witting statement offered by the supervisee drawn from this communication, and then there is another level of expression that is seeking recognition and may come regularly into the spiral of recognition.
2. The ability to be able to hold certain experiences together as complementary in the supervision dialogue. Being able to contain both thoughts and feelings for the supervisee in such a manner that they may be addressed again at the appropriate moment in time and context. Encountered again in the spiral of learning. Sometimes this is recognized as a parallel process.
3. Working in a spirit of abstinence so that the working session is devoted to the needs of the supervisee and the presented client or group of clients. Remaining alert to the personal clamouring for self-expression that exists in all of us, and inhibiting it when the need arises to do so, but not to the point where we lose our essential humanity.
4. Remaining alert to the whole context of the supervision material so that potentially conflicting claims for attention are not treated in a rivalrous manner, but are properly recognized and attended to satisfactorily.
5. Being willing to provide information drawn from the rich bed of experience in the possession of the supervisor. Responding to the needs of the

supervisee by offering clear support at the right moment, when it can be of most use to the supervisee. Finding the right moment is the imperative.

6. Paying close attention to the supervisee's emotional internal world to help her respond to personal feelings in a way that is beneficial to her and her client.

7. Remembering, and working with, the basic assumption of the first priority: the well-being and safety of the client or group of clients in their relationship with the therapist.

8. Keeping well informed in the theory and practice of the therapy/counselling mode being practised by the supervisee in order to understand and to be a provider of appropriate ideas when these may be required in the supervision relationship.

9. Providing a secure, undisturbed and attractive setting for supervision which is compatible with the serious nature of the supervision activity.

10. Providing a regular structure of supervision sessions that is appropriate to the needs of the supervisee and within the competence and availability of the supervisor.

No doubt readers could add to this list, but it seems to me to represent the basic conditions, which may need expansion or modification depending upon to the particular situation of supervisor and supervisee.

The experience of 'bad' supervision is often concerned with the structure and timing of sessions and the supervisor not keeping to her undertakings to see and meet at agreed times and places. Good rituals need to be constructed and observed. In earlier chapters I have described concerns about abuse occurring in different ways, and the concern that all supervisors need to exhibit in recognizing the essential power imbalance of the supervision situation.

I think it's important to briefly discuss the question of money and the provision of supervision by private practitioners. I have already discussed earlier in the book some of the problems that arise when supervision is in-house. Boundaries and the issue of authority and the real possibility of 'reporting back' to higher authorities certainly come into play as issues when institutional supervision is provided. In certain professions this is simply accepted as part and parcel of the professional culture. In social work, for example, there are a number of forms of supervision – be they managerial or professional – especially where casework is being practised.

Where the clinical supervision of psychotherapy and counselling is 'placed outside' the employing body such problems diminish. But who should pay? There is no such thing as a free lunch.

My own experience has been mixed. One supervisee some years ago paid me out of her own pocket to supervise work she was carrying out in a GP practice. The practice would not meet her expenses in this respect or provide appropriate in-house supervision. Fortunately, at least two employers in my present supervision practice meet my professional fees. One employer pays me £35 per session, the other £40 per session. I am glad that two employers have seen the correctness of this provision, and I am especially pleased that a traditional NHS hospital is one of them.

Other questions arise, in particular those concerning the presence of religious and social beliefs and political convictions and how these impact upon the world of therapeutic/counselling supervision. Our personal belief systems are highly influential in our lives and constitute powerfully influential features of our being, especially in our choice of human relationships. Bearing this in mind, it should be relatively easily recognized that clinical supervisors should not be brought into the assessment procedures of psychotherapy or counselling training courses. Where, unfortunately, this happens, it is quite obvious that the relationship between supervisor and supervisee is going to be seriously undermined to the detriment of both.

The training of supervisors would certainly not be conducted in a 'value free' context. On the contrary, their training would almost certainly contain both conscious and unconscious elements of judgement that would probably be assimilated without much challenge by the trainees. If the reader doubts this, I would simply ask her to notice how deferential we are, as a profession, to the expertise of our 'betters' when we attend lectures and seminars. I notice, with a feeling of unease, how, when scribbling in our notebooks, we are reluctant to enter into debate. I suppose we are all intimidated to some extent by the expertise of others and by our own tentative knowledge.

To answer my own question, I feel I have to come down on the side of training for supervisors with the caveat that it should not be determined by a curriculum and method laid down by our present governing institutions: both academic and professional. In my view we would benefit from a diversity of training initiatives, afforded by trainers who hold dear certain professional principles of supervision. From these we can take our pick to suit our disposition and belief system. I am quite sure that a unified, centrally controlled supervision training curriculum would do nothing but harm to our professions. Let us have the best of both worlds: freedom and responsibility.

# Conclusion

This book has been written not because of my intrinsic interest in the subject or because of my experience as a supervisor, but because I have grown aware of a movement in the world of trainers, in particular towards a conception of supervision as a model of didactic learning. The focus is upon the trainee supervisor learning from, and through, their supervisors within a hierarchical structure of learner and teacher. The nature of that learning is set in an educational framework, and the proposed relationship between supervisee and supervisor is that of student and teacher.

This view of the supervisor and the trainer is also associated with psychotherapy and counselling training organizations, where the role of supervision is incorporated into the training process judgementally (Fonagy, 2000). Thus the special independent position of the role of supervisor is likely to be seriously undermined and with it the quality of the relationship with psychotherapy and supervision trainees. I am sure this position must undermine the clinical work and independence of the trainee and supervisor alike. It could be argued that elements of the hierarchical structure can be justified in the training situation, although I would be very unhappy for it to become the rule. It strikes me as altogether inappropriate, beyond the initial training situation, for this learning construct to be offered to the experienced supervisee and the supervisor, both of whom are skilled and sophisticated practitioners.

Thus I have formulated the concept of the relationship (both intellectual and emotional) between supervisee and therapist/counsellor as being based upon a dynamic and equally respected position of learning, and which can be used to the benefit of the presented client or group. This is usually called the relational approach, and I hope I have influenced the reader to give it serious consideration as a viable and supportable form of supervision to be enjoyed by supervisor and supervisee alike.

As far as training goes, as yet there is no national register of 'recognized' supervisor training courses for psychotherapists and counsellors. However,

135

there are some courses that have limited recognition and may in time come to be recognized by the UKCP.

*Dramatherapists* should contact:

Marina Jenkyns, Course Director, Ditty Dokter, associated lecturer, Supervisors Training Course.
Enquiries: 21a Southcote Rd, London N19 5BJ
Tel: 0207 609 1728

A privately run course recognized as proficient by the British Association of Dramatherapists.There may well be a privately run course in the supervision of psychodramatists, but as yet I am unaware of such a provision.

## BAPPS

Within the last few years a body called the British Association for Psychoanalytic and Psychodynamic Supervision has come into being. The BAPPS is a member of the UKCP (PPP Section) and has been set up to draw up a list of supervisors working within its criteria for membership. In this sense they are accredited not usually by training but more often by experience as therapists and counsellors; all of them are registered with either:

1.  The United Kingdom Council for Psychotherapy,
2.  The British Confederation of Psychotherapists, or are
3.  accredited members of the British Association for Counselling & Psychotherapy

The BAPPS publishes a list of their members, which may be obtained on application to:

PO Box 275, Dorking. Surrey, RH4 1YR
E-mail: bapad@adbapps.freeserve.co.uk

It should be noted that the BAPPS is not a training organization.

## Westminster Pastoral Foundation. North.

A new course was launched in September 2001 by the WPF.North.

1.  Diploma in Psychodynamic and Psychoanalytic Supervision
2.  One-year Course
3.  Starts in September 2001

Contact: Jean Bradley, WPF Counselling North, Leeds Bridge House, Hunslet Road, Leeds, LS10 1JN.
Tel: 0113 245 0303.
E-mail: wpf.north@dial.pipex.com

Counsellors may wish to explore training in supervision with **CASCADE** Training Associates.They offer a variety of supervisor developmental courses, residential or local.
Enquiries: 42, Holland Street, Brighton, BN2 2WB.

As I was concluding this book I came across an article in the *British Journal of Guidance and Counselling* (Vol 27, No 2) by David King and Sue Wheeler (1999), entitled 'The responsibilities of counsellor supervisors: a qualitative study'.

It is a tightly argued discussion of the nature of supervision and its pitfalls. Although I do not share the view of the authors that a survey of only ten people produces totally convincing evidence, I nevertheless strongly recommend it to all readers. What it has to say is mostly applicable to therapists of all disciplines. It makes for a good read.

A final word. It occurred to me in my preparation for this book that it would be a good idea to approach a number of supervisees, most of whom experienced supervision with me and other supervisors, and ask them to reflect on what they were looking for in supervision.

I gave them no further guidance and simply asked for about 500 words on the subject, drawn entirely from their own expectations and experience.

I am very pleased because they all replied, and their contributions to this book appears in 'Reflections' immediately after this chapter.

Thank you, all of you.

**Don Feasey**

# Reflections

## What I look for in supervision

### Dr Douglas Fraser

*Psychoanalytic Psychotherapist*

My first thought when considering what I look for in supervision was to think about safety. Never quite able perhaps to set aside my analytic hat, such a thought led to a reflection about whether I looked for safety as a means of warding off a sense of the unsafe: a sense that placing oneself before the supervisory gaze might put something in jeopardy. It struck me that my immediate concern was about protecting something, and that part of what was most important here was to do with safeguarding: maintaining a kind of loyalty to what made possible the relationship in which my patient and myself were participants. What I'm driving at here has to do with value and valuing. The value I bestow and go on investing in work with someone emerges as an articulation of the relationship itself. It forms a rubric that makes work possible. Consequently, what I look for in a supervision turns on my question: will there be sufficient valuing of my valuing – sufficient to enable a supervisor to stand back in a kind of willing awe and respect of the relationship experience I bring? An evenly hovering attention on its own won't do. What is rather needed here is a passion of interest that is delighted with its object of investigation and is a little in awe of it. When I have the opportunity to talk to someone about someone I'm working with, I want them to feel this passion, which includes a sense of privilege, for that will enable me to preserve *my* passion for articulation.

That might sound a long-winded way of rather more simply saying: when I go for supervision, I want attention, albeit a special kind of attention. But this way of putting things again won't do. Attention itself is too general, and in any case we must account for what grounds it. The theoreticians and modellers of consciousness have barely begun, let alone finished their reduc-

138

tions. Neither do I much care for the term 'supervision'. It smacks of expert, of Archimedian viewpoints posturing the promise of some totalizing 'super' account. Our world is full of 'super'; look at our world! There is a long-standing debate in NHS psychotherapy circles, in which I work, about the distinction between supervision and consultation and what that means for clinical responsibility. Perhaps a new term will emerge which will ditch the 'super'. Perhaps next year I'll be able to schedule part of my week to include simply 'vision', or, better, 'co-vision'.

When we are seduced by the 'super', covision is disabled and the potential of the relationship is compromised. The mistake of trying to grasp the patient instead of the supervisee's relation with the patient, a (super) tendency we can all – as supervisors – move in and out of, is one example of such a compromise. Here a kind of theft can subtly impose itself whereby in the name of a mastering discourse the therapist in a real sense can find himself relieved of his patient – a move which, of course, supervisees themselves can be complicit in. As a clinician and supervisor I have learned that supervisees require certain conditions of possibility to be observed and valued for good work to ensue. Such conditions include feeling valued for the work one has chosen to do. Feeling valued is a necessary condition for our capacity to value ourselves and our patients. A treatment that can renew or restore a patient's access to feeling better is impossible otherwise. Experiencing safety as a constituent property of such valuing can evoke in the supervisee a recuperative, replenishing experience whereby the work of gathering insight, refining sense and meaning, coming into touch with a greater range of therapeutic positions in a given case, can become a pleasure, a passion.

Moving from giving therapy to receiving conditions of possibility for vision involves a move from one culture to another. There are points of resemblance, affinities.

But they are different. Good 'supervision' – which is what we all look for – will enhance such a move and make it into a glide, leaving us perhaps feeling super!

February 2001

## Ye Min

*Dramatherapist/Psychotherapist*

I have been working in special needs teaching since 1982, and not long after qualifying I became interested in the creative therapies. I began my dramatherapy training when I was a teacher at a residential school for children with autism. A requirement of that course was that I undertook supervision, and ever since 1990 I have been involved in that process.

Since that time I have had four supervisors. The first sessions were one to one, and later there was group supervision with either one or two other therapists. Looking back, I am aware of the specialized nature of my job and how this has influenced my supervision needs.

In the beginning, as a dramatherapy student, supervision was a time to share the anxieties and receive some guidance about theory and technique. I was also staggered by the fact that, unlike teacher training, my supervisor would not be observing me. My supervisor would take my word for whatever I chose to share, and the skill of the supervisor would look beneath what I said and intuitively discover the subtext.

Later on, as a practising dramatherapist, I was involved in a three-way supervision model. My co-supervisees were not working in education and this highlighted the difficulty of what seemed to be working in an isolated and specialized field, i.e. a residential school for children with autism. The skill of the supervisor would highlight the differences and similarities and use them as focus for reflective discussion about the issues we had each raised as individuals. In that way we were able to voice our needs, but it also gave us an insight into our colleagues' situation to discover whether there was a common ground of practice.

The length of the session was also more than the hour normally allocated for a one-to-one supervision.

Now I am working peripatetically as a dramatherapist in mainstream schools. We have had two supervisors during the three years of this practice. Neither of them has a specialization within our field, and only one was a dramatherapist. However, both have a wide experience of therapeutic work and supervision.

In the same way that we consider what the clients' need are in therapy, we as therapists have to consider what our needs are in supervision. I have discovered a new way to move forward. I have come to believe that, as in therapy, the supervisor has to demonstrate listening skills and the ability to contain and provide a safe environment. The supervisor has to have a broad therapeutic outlook that can accommodate the supervisee's specialism. I also feel that the supervisor has to generate a confidence that will allow the supervisee to feel that they are understood and that their needs are contained.

The important point about being understood is that I feel working as a therapist within the education system there appears to be a completely different system of hierarchies, boundaries, confidentiality and rights issues than there would be within the health service. On reflection, I realize how my supervision needs have changed through the years and this is evident in the issues I may raise within the session. I expect the supervisor to use their skill and expertise to allow me to creatively explore the parts of my therapeutic practice that are causing me concern. With the supervisor's objective outlook I hope to be able to reflect upon my practice and discover a new way forward.

February 2001

## Mary Cox M.Ed

*UKCP Registered Psychotherapist*
*Teaching and Supervising Transactional Analyst (Clinical)*

Over twenty-five years of practice I have developed and changed my use of supervision through several stages; my needs have been different at each stage. However, at all stages a primary concern is to have a supervisor who is well boundaried, ethical and provides a 'safe' place in which I can discuss freely issues related to any of my professional activities.

As a novice therapist I looked for practical guidance and teaching on 'what to do' and 'how to do it' together with lots of reassurance from my supervisor. I needed patience, evident experience that I could trust and an ability to give negative feedback clearly without being critical.

As I became more experienced I wanted help with translating models and theories into practice with clients in a way that helped me to learn how to find some answers to my questions using my own understanding. I wanted help in learning how to 'meta-think'.

Then during the long period of practice as a regular full-time psychotherapist I found I wanted two main things. First, help with identifying counter-transference, which was almost always the source of a clinical problem, and, second, I wanted personal support and backup, especially with regard to any ethical and professional issues that might have arisen.

In my final professional stage as a psychotherapy trainer and supervisor what I want from my supervisor is intelligent listening, experienced reflection, realistic mirroring, perceptive confrontation and a sense of personal warmth and humour. These all contribute to the creation of a reliable time and place and relationship within which I feel supported professionally and which helps me to avoid the twin dangers of professional arrogance and isolation. I look for a relationship that is both collegial and one that I can 'lean on' when I feel the need.

February 2001

## Roz Cran

*Counsellor. BAC accredited*

During a decade of counselling I have experienced working with four supervisors and being a member of two supervision groups, one led by a tutor while I was a trainee, and latterly being in a peer group.

As a trainee undertaking an advanced diploma course and on placement at a university counselling service I was lucky enough to have a placement supervisor and to be part of a supervision group at college, which met weekly for half a day.

At the group we took turns to listen to our taped sessions for which we would have prepared; the tutor would comment and other members of the group could add observations. A good learning forum.

With my placement supervisor at a fortnightly session I could discuss people I was working with, bring questions and concerns. As a trainee it felt easy to say 'I don't know' or 'I feel unqualified to help this person'. Later, as a qualified and experienced counsellor, I still need to say this at times, and supervision is the only place to do it. It is extremely important to me to know I have a place to unburden.

Both these first supervision places felt safe and supportive, and I could let out my worries and know that those listening would try to understand and help me to resolve my queries in a useful way. Both mirrored what I hoped to provide as a counsellor: a safe place to explore difficulties but in this case focussed on my work as a counsellor.

After I qualified, the supervisor at my placement agreed to continue and supported me for a couple of years through a variety of counselling posts. When she decided to leave counselling and supervision, I felt panicky and wondered whether I could find another such supervisor. I am sure this also mirrors the feelings many clients feel as they move towards the end of counselling. I was able to find another supervisor and make the transition while still seeing my first supervisor. This helped me enormously; I felt looked after and had no gap in supervision.

I soon built up a good relationship with my second supervisor, a counselling psychologist, who was a very different personality but whom I trusted and was able to share my concerns and who appreciated my qualities, which in turn helped me to recognize my value as a counsellor. I worked with her for five years. She saw me through the BAC accreditation process in 1994.

During this time I took on work in an NHS Trust, in a clinical psychology service. Here I had internal supervision from a clinical psychologist and, when she became my line manager, from another psychologist. Both of these people had some training in counselling, one was an ex-Relate counsellor who had trained in clinical psychology, and the other had some psychodynamic training. Both were very supportive and helpful and shared their experience with me.

After taking a year out and moving south, I have returned to counselling within an NHS psychology and counselling service and now have supervision in a peer group, consisting of me and four or five clinical psychologists. This is a very different experience. I have to share the time instead of having one-and-a-half hours to myself. I learn a lot from hearing them discuss their work. They are supportive. But I miss having that one-to-one relationship with a supervisor. Also I have to listen and try and make helpful suggestions. I am working in the time I am used to having for myself.

As a counselling supervisor for several years I have been on the other end of the relationship. I have supported trainee and qualified counsellors. I experienced a sense of responsibility to their clients, to monitor that the counsellors were working ethically and competently. This once-removed relationship is complex. But I enjoyed discussing their work and supporting these counsellors.

My chief feeling about supervision is the tremendous help that comes from supportive relationships: how much better I worked and how much better others must work when they feel safe to work creatively to take the risks involved in developing their practice.

December 2000

### Martin Gill

*Psychodrama Psychotherapist, Dramatherapist*
*BPA, BAD, UKCP*

Gender choice and dual qualification of dramatherapy and psychodrama became deciding factors for me after the death of my father, which led me to choose a male supervisor who was dual trained in both modalities.

I chose to work with Don Feasey in a small, all-male group, which took place in his cosy living room in a large suburban Edwardian family house. I enjoyed this male support, and I negotiated two sessions back-to-back to supervise my dramatherapy and psychodrama practice. In retrospect I negotiated a contract where I had more time than the other supervisees who were trained in a single modality. Because by this stage I was more experienced I at times took on a more advisory role with the other supervisees, which brings questions to my mind about group issues and supervision (the need for supervision for supervision!).

I'm sure that Don has addressed some of these issues in this book. Don's 'style' of supervision, although he came from a psychodynamic background, was quite anecdotal and friendly, which again satisfied my need for both a colleague and experienced guide. In retrospect I feel that, as a supervisee, I needed to be more aware of these issues and deciding factors in choosing him and how this might have affected the transference material I brought to the supervision. I'm aware that over the past few years there has been more training available for supervisors in dramatherapy. I feel this is a further positive step in bringing the profession forwards. My hope is that latter-day training courses have the opportunity to educate trainees in some of the relationship issues new practitioners face.

Over the past three years I've been working with an *in situ* team-supervision method in the use of psychodrama. This has been part of a model called 'Therapeutic Spiral' and was devised by a number of international clinicians under the direction of psychodramatist and clinical psychologist Dr Kate Hudgins. It is a clinical application of psychodrama for working with trauma survivors. Supervision takes place as an integral dynamic part of the work. After working with clients as a team leader, assistant or auxiliary the team members timetable a space to process their actions/responses, countertransference and personal issues together. For me, this 'at the time' approach to supervision has been an exciting new approach, both as a professional practitioner and for my own personal development.

February 2001

### Moira Goddard

*BAC accredited UKRC Registered Independent Counsellor*

When I was a new counsellor, more years ago than I care to count, I had a firm belief (shared by many new counsellors) that all supervisors had a supervisor who was cleverer than they were and that that supervisor had an even more experienced supervisor, and so the ladder went on, reaching into the heavens, until, at last, it reached the God of supervision. I suppose that when I realized that that wasn't true was when I began to grow up in counselling terms.

So what do I want from my supervisor now when I no longer want or expect him to be God?

First of all I want a safe place where I can bring my work. I need to be able to share the pleasure of successful outcomes, but also to bring the aspects of the work that cause me concern. Nowadays that is less about the clients' concerns and more about my concerns with the client. It is important to be able to share perspectives, to reflect on my interventions and to explore alternative ways of working. My countertransference thoughts and feelings, together with those of my supervisor, are positive ways of shedding new light on stuck situations.

I need to feel valued and to believe that my supervisor has confidence in the way that I work, and that enables me to be stimulated and encouraged by the challenges that supervision brings in our work together.

For me, Winnicott still best sums up supervision:

> The good-enough counsellor can survive the negative attacks of the client through the strength of being held in the supervisory relationship. The supervisor's role is not just to reassure the worker but to allow the emotional disturbance to be felt in

the safer setting of the supervisory relationship where it can be survived, reflected upon and learnt from. Supervision thus provides a container that holds the helping relationship within the therapeutic triad.

The longer I work in counselling and supervision, the more one thing becomes clear to me. There is no one best model in counselling, any more than there is one route to God. Yes, theory and process are important, and we need to be sure of what we are doing and why, but just as the most valuable tool that the counsellor can bring to her clients is herself in the therapeutic relationship, so it is with counsellor and supervisor. I need to be in tune with my supervisor even when we don't agree with each other. I need him to know me and what is going on in my life well enough so that he can be aware of my countertransference issues. The words 'that's not like you, Moira' give me food for reflection and understanding. Also preserve me from a supervisor who can't laugh; a sense of humour is a vital aspect with what, at times, can feel an intolerable load.

So three cheers for the good-enough supervisor, the good-enough counsellor and the good-enough client; we have the potential to do some good work together.

PS. I have used the word 'he' when referring to my supervisor because my current supervisor happens to be a man.

February 2001

**Eileen MacAlister**

*Group Analyst and Psychotherapist*

I have worked for many years as a therapist and had experience of a number of different approaches to client material within a clinical supervision setting.

Among the qualities I most look for when choosing a supervisor is their ability to engage with my particular style when I am operating as a therapist and also their understanding about the manner in which I work. I believe that the supervisor's greater understanding of these aspects of me will support me in my work and ultimately will lead to a more successful outcome for my clients.

While I want the supervisory relationship to be challenging, it is important to me that the supervisor has a good understanding of systems theory and can hold any organizational setting where I may be working 'in mind'. I am especially concerned with this aspect of the relationship with the supervisor because I am aware that the therapist can encourage a too rarefied atmosphere in the consulting room where reality can become minimized or at times even lost. Then, within the framework of their understanding of the system, I would expect that the supervisor could use a reflective process to help me develop my understanding of transferential and countertransferential issues.

It seems to me that, by knowing me well, the supervisor is enabled to identify some of the less accessible aspects of what occurs in the actual therapy sessions. For instance, if the psychopathology of my client subtly encourages or even seduces me to work in a manner that differs from my usual style, it is essential for me to develop a conscious awareness of this affect. The supervisor can enable this to become conscious allowing me to think more clearly both about the case as a whole and also specifically about what psychological defences may be operating in the consulting room.

As within therapy, the potential for abuse within supervision is always present. I believe it is essential that the supervisor has a clear sense regarding the boundaries between that which should be taken into the supervisee's personal therapy and that which may require amplification within the supervision session. When working with aspects of countertransference, this area is often murky and therefore the skill and sensitivity of the supervisor is paramount to ensure a good enough holding environment is created both for the supervisee and their client.

Briefly considering only one or two important aspects of supervision reminds me again of the level of responsibility that the supervisor carries and the necessity of the supervisor themselves having a safe place to reflect upon this work.

February 2001

## From....A. [who wishes to remain anonymous]

*An experienced psychotherapist and counsellor*

Thinking about what I want in supervision, I have imagined what would be useful in a session. It might go something like this:

I come prepared to describe a session with a patient. In an earlier meeting with my supervisor I have talked about the work with this person, and so we focus on the current therapeutic work, and I use notes I have made immediately after the session with the patient. Although the account includes details of the interaction, it does not plan or structure what I will say.

The supervisor listens without interruption to my account of a session and then makes comments or asks questions. He may contrast a beneficial interpretation I have made with one which was poor, or make a general observation about what happened. He will also repeat and reflect on some of the patient's words and behaviours.

This is rather like an introduction to our exploration of the session in all its aspects: the transferential and countertransferential parts of the relationship, what we think the patient may mean, what I mean, the dilemmas and the puzzling features.

If this part is freeflowing, reflective and I trust the supervisory relationship, the supervisor, guided by his own experience in the session, may identify something that has been difficult for me to put into words. He may make a suggestion, recommendation or warn me about a potential problem or risk to the client.

I recognize at the time that this is significant because of the strong emotional impact on me. Often it is surprising. It may take a few minutes or several hours to bring it into insight, making links in my mind between the therapeutic session and the supervision.

The end point is usually realizing what is particularly painful for the patient – the terror or shame, for instance, she has experienced, which has been hard for me to hold in my head (the reasons to do with me or with the patient).

The most useful part of a supervision session is about being enabled, in a safe way, to look squarely at whatever is deeply troubling to the patient.

February 2001

## Ann Howarth

*Registered Psychotherapist*

Over past 20 years I have been supervised by seven supervisors on an individual basis. I can think of many words to describe my needs from a supervisor over this period of time, such as mentor, role model, container and a supporter of my work. Implicit in this alliance has been trust, tolerance, new learning, confidence building with tactful intervention, attention to the transference and countertransference processes, empathic connectedness and recognition from colleagues, all of which have been essential in my growth as a therapist.

However, my enduring need has been for a supervisor who has more experience than I have and who can empathize with and challenge my psychodynamic psychoanalytical orientation. I need to feel safe to explore my own thought processes and to be able to expose my innermost, sometimes frightening, feelings, which I know are causing the impasse, such that at times they can render me feeling hopeless, lacking in confidence and doubtful about my theoretical knowledge. This containment in supervision has been a key factor in my ability to hold almost unbearable, often confusing, feelings that can emerge in the therapy session in the interpersonal process between me and the patient.

Primarily, I need to trust that the transference and countertransference issues can be understood before any critical or empathic interventions are forthcoming from my supervisor. If the supervisor is initially too much in the foreground with his/her anxiety to understand the patient, this does not allow me space to enter the patient's world or my experience of the patient.

This space enables me to replicate the same unconscious attitudes and dilemmas created within the therapy session in the parallel process of supervision. I find that I gain more illumination of the process when I talk it through with my supervisor. In this way I often realize my omissions and the missing links that I have not previously explored. I usually become aware, when I want my supervisor to provide answers for me, that these are the demands of my patient in defence of their hopelessness.

I value also the ability of my supervisor to work with metaphor and dreams as a way of accessing and understanding more of the unconscious process, particularly in very resistant patients. I find it helpful to have a third ear that is removed from the interference of the countertransference which might highlight some of the differences and similarities between the patient's interpretation and my own. Recently, a patient who splits off his emotional self from sex and has difficulty seeing me as a woman (even more, a sexual woman), recounted one of his dreams:

We were in my study, and I was wearing a black evening dress with a wrap around my shoulders. Suddenly, I jumped up, whereupon the wrap dropped to the floor. The patient recalls backing away in his chair.

This patient is prone to secrecy in his personal life. He has perpetuated this in his therapy by being, at times, extremely withholding, almost inviting me to force him into submission like his punishing, yet exciting, mother. In working with the thoughts of 'wraps', 'keeping things under wraps' and 'what was under the wrap', my supervisor mentioned the word 'illicit'. Immediately I was able to make the connection that I had missed in my interpretation, i.e. that he was unable to see me as a sexual woman. Indeed, I began to realize that I had become the predatory female from whom there was no escape, like his mother. This dynamic had definitely touched on my defence against anxiety of being an active sexual woman rather than the recipient of a sexual fantasy.

The revelation, which has been nurtured by the many aspects of supervision I have mentioned, is the power of the countertransference as the patient tries to recreate his/her familiar world. Importantly, I now accept that I do not need to know everything, and that two minds working for the common cause of the patient's mental health can unlock the creativity of both.

February 2001

## Ann Haworth has the last word, shifting her perspective to that of suprevisor

My first task as a supervisor is to assess the experience of the supervisee because this will inevitably determine the level at which I supervise. I make it clear that my style is psychodynamic, analytical and that I often pay attention to the parallel process.

I am usually far more active with less experienced supervisees in that I am more engaged with the structure of the session and holding the supervisee. Personally, if a client is being presented for the first time even by an experienced supervisee, I like to know about certain facts and realities in much the same way. I need to know about the referral, by whom and what has been expressed about the client, and why now. If I am working with an experienced supervisee I am more apt to let the material unfold, perhaps asking a question at an appropriate time in line with the supervisee's thoughts if the external realities of the client's history and symptoms are not forthcoming. I also focus on the client's needs and whether this compares with any that might have been stated by the referrer. If any contract has been made, I like to know whether this has had to be confined or not by the working environment, the institute, the request of the client or the needs of the supervisee. Sometimes I find supervisees who prefer to offer six sessions and then a review, but then keep repeating this process rather than working with an open-ended contract, even if they are not confined by the number of sessions offered. I tend to discourage this practice, particularly if a client has a history of recurrent losses or a series of uncommitted relationships. It seems stability is required, even though this might raise anxiety levels in the first instance.

Throughout I am very tuned into my feelings about the client, often taking cues from the way in which the supervisee presents the material. However, I store this information until I hear how the supervisee experiences the patient in the session. This information is much more easily elicited from an experienced counsellor, as, generally, inexperienced ones are too anxiously tied up with detail and their skills practice to be able to grasp hold of these feelings in the session. Gradually, they can be explored retrospectively in supervision with the developing confidence and growth of the supervisee. I constantly listen for underlying themes in the clients' relationships so that we can begin to forecast the likely defensive manoeuvres that will be acted in or out of the therapy. This was very evident in two assessment sessions a supervisee recently brought to me. Throughout the presentations the theme of the clients' relationships was about expectations placed on her by others and which she could not fulfil. When the supervisee discussed the limited contract and the focus with which the client had agreed, it was obvious that the same dilemma had been set up. Interestingly, the supervisee said, 'I think I am expecting too much of her.' As I helped her think about the themes, the supervisee began to realize that she was experiencing the countertransference in which she had become unwittingly involved.

When a supervisee brings an impasse to me, I encourage them to reflect on what they might do now instead. The more experienced the supervisee, the more able they are to use this space creatively away from the anxiety of the client and to tolerate not knowing as opposed to feeling defensive, criticized or put on the spot. The supervisee is sometimes horrified to find out how ambivalent they feel towards their client and how this can be the cause of their 'stuckness'. Once this is able to be voiced and explored further in supervision, it seems to be unconsciously conveyed to the next therapy session, at which the impasse seems magically to disappear.

Supervision is an essential part of every counsellor's or psychotherapist's work programme. Hopefully, within a developing relationship between supervisor and supervisee the sessions can move from nervous anticipation of doubt and lack of confidence to a more exciting place, imbibing more knowledge, skills and creativity.

February 2001

# References

Argyle M  (1969) Social Interaction. London: Methuen.

Argyle M et al. (1970) The communication of inferior and superior attitudes by verbal and non-verbal signals. Brit Journal Clin.Psychol. Vol 91. pp 222–231.

Ashurst P (1993) Supervision of the Beginning Therapist. British Journal of Psychotherapy. Vol 10. No 3 pp 170–177.

Aveline M and Dryden W (Eds) (1988) Group Therapy in Britain. Oxford: OUP.

BACUP (1996) BACUP Code of Ethics an Practice for Supervisors of Counsellors, Rugby.

Barnes B, Ernst S and Hyde K (1999) An Introduction to Group Work. London: Macmillan.

Bernard J (1994) Multicultural supervision. Counseller Education and Supervision. Vol 34. pp 159–71.

Beryce W Maclennan (1970) Group Counselling. Columbia: UP.

Bion W (1961) Experiences in Groups. New York: Basic Books.

Bott P (1979) Systems Model for Group Supervision. Group Analysis 12 (2) p134.

Brecht B (1998) Messingkauf Dialogues. London: Routledge.

British Association of Counselling and Psychotherapy (2000) Information Sheet No.8.

Brown D and Peddar (1979) Introduction to Psychotherapy. London: Tavistock.

Brown JAC (1950) The Social Psychology of Industry. Harmondsworth: Penguin.

Burton E J (1955) Drama in Schools. London: Herbert Jenkins.

Carroll M and Holloway E (1999) Counselling Supervision in Context. London: Sage.

Carroll M and Holloway E (1999) Training Counselling Supervisors: Strategies, Models and Methods London: Sage pp 44–65.

Carroll M (1995) The Generic Tasks of Supervision. PhD. Dissertation University of Surrey.

Carroll M (1996) Counselling Supervision: Theory, Skills and Practice. London: Cassell.

Clark W (1982) Freud. A Biography. London: Granada Publishing Ltd.

Clarkson P (1995) The Therapeutic Relationship. London: Whurr.

Clarkson P (1997) The Bystander (An End to Innocence in Human Relationships). London: Whurr.

Clegg D in Pemberton-Billing RN and Clegg D (1965) Teaching Drama. London: University of London Press.

Coltart N (1993) How to Survive as a Psychotherapist. London: Sheldon Press.

de Board R (1978) The Psychoanalysis of Organizations. London: Tavistock.

Dowrick C (1996) Sole bearers: reflections from a Balint group. Changes Vol 14. No 2.

Dryden W (Ed) (1984) Individual Psychotherapy in Britain. London: Harper and Row.

Edwards D (1997) Supervision today in Shipton ed. Supervision of Psychotherapy and Counselling. Buckingham: Open University Press. pp 11-23.

Ekstein R (1964) Psychotherapy: Theory, Research and Practice, Vol 1. pp 137-138.

Feasey D (1972) Working with Youth. London: BBC Publications.

Feasey D (1996) The Experience of Supervision. Journal of the WMIP. Vol 15. No 1. pp 29-40.

Feasey D (1998) Will It or Won't It Work ? Changes Vol 16. No 2. pp 92-104.

Feasey D (1999) Good Practice in Counselling and Psychotherapy. London: Whurr.

Feasey D (2000) Good Practice in Psychodrama: an Analytic Perspective. London: Whurr.

Feltham C (1999) Baselines, problems and possibilities in Taking Supervision Forward eds. Lawton L and Feltham C. London: Sage.

Fine R (1992) Supervision and the Analytic Ego in Psychoanalytic Approaches to Analytic Supervision. New York: Brunner Mazel.

Fletcher J (1966) Situation Ethics: The New Morality. London: SCM Press.

Fletchman B (1993). British patients of Caribbean origin. British Journal of Psychotherapy, Vol 10. No 1.

Fonagy P. (2000) The future of psychoanalysis. The Psycotherapist no.15, pp 30-33.

Fordham M (1982) How Do I Assess Progress in Supervision? Symposium. Journal of Analytical Psychology 27. pp 110-113.

Foulkes SH (1948) Introduction to Group-Analytic Psychotherapy. London: Maresfield reprints.

Foulkes SH (1975) Group Analytic Psychotherapy. London: Gordon and Breach.

Freud S (1926) On the Question of Lay Analysis. Standard Edition. Pelican Freud Library No. 15 from 1973.

Garrard A and Wiles J (1957) Leap to Life. London: Chatto and Windus.

Goldie L (1986) Psychoanalysis in the NHS General Hospital. Psychoanalytic Psychotherapy Vol 1. No 2.

Golding W (1954) Lord of the Flies. London: Faber and Faber.

Hawkins P and Shohet R (1989) Supervision in the Helping Professions. Milton Keynes: Open University Press.

Holloway EL (1995) Clinical Supervision. A Systems Approach. Thousand Oaks, California: Sage.

Holloway EL and Carroll M (eds) (1999) Training Counselling Supervisors. London: Sage

Holmes P (1992) The Inner World Outside. London: Routledge

Holmes J (1999) in Barnes, Ernst and Hyde (Eds) (1999) An Introduction to Group Work. London: Macmillan.

Inskipp F (1996) New directions in supervision in Bayne, Horton and Bimrose, eds. New Directions in Counselling. London: Routledge.

Inskipp F and Proctor B (1995) Becoming a Supervisor. Vol 2. Twickenham: Cascade.

Jenkyns M (1999) Supervision and Dramatherapy Tselikas-Portmann (Ed.) pp 186. London: Jessica Kingsley.

Jennings S (1981) Remedial Drama. London: A & C Black.

Jennings S (1990) Dramatherapy with Groups, Families and Individuals. London: Jessica Kingsley.

Johnson DR (1992) The dramatherapist in-role in Dramatherapy: Theory and Practice. Ed. Sue Jennings. London: Routledge.

Jones E (1957) Sigmund Freud Vol 3. London: Hogarth Press

Kaberry S (2000) In Taking Supervision Forward. Part 1. Chapter 3. pp 42–60. Lawton B and Feltham C Eds. London: Sage Publications.

Karp M and Holmes P (1991) Psychodrama Inspiration and Technique. London: Routledge.

Kennard D (1998) An Introduction to Therapeutic Communities. London: Jessica Kingsley.

King D. and Wheeler S (1999) The responsibilities of counsellor supervisors: a qualitative study. Brit. Journal of Guidance and Counselling. Vol 27. No 2.

Klein M (1975) Envy and Gratitude and Other Works: 1946–63. New York: Delacourt.

Kovel J (1982) A Complete Guide to Therapy. London: Pelican Books.

Landy R (1992) One to One in Dramatherapy: Theory and Practice, Ed. Sue Jennings. London: Routledge.

Lawton L and Feltham C (Eds) (2000) Taking Supervision Forward. London: Sage.

Lewin K (1952) Field Theory in Social Science. London: Tavistock.

Maclennan W (1966) in Group dynamics in a supervisory group of students learning psychotherapy, in: The International Handbook of Group Psychotherapy ed. JL Moreno. London: Peter Owen.

Malan DH (1979) Individual Psychotherapy and the Science of Psychodynamics. London: Butterworths.

Masson J (1992) Final Analysis. London: Fontana.

Mitchell SA (1988) Relational Concepts. Harvard University Press.

Mitchell SA (1995) Hope and Dread in Psychoanalysis. New York: Basic Books.

Moodley R (1999) Psychotherapy with ethnic minorities. Changes Vol 17. No 2. p 109.

Moreno JL (1946) Psychodrama and Group Psychotherapy. New York: Beacon.

Moreno JL (Ed) (1966) International Handbook of Group Psychotherapy. London: Peter Owen.

Newnes C, Holmes G and Dunn C (Eds) (1999) This is Madness. Ross-on-Wye: PCCS Books.

Newton G (1937) Acting Improvised. London: Nelson and Son.

Pedder J (1986) Psychoanalytic Psychotherapy. Vol 2. No 1. pp 1–12.

Pemberton-Billing RN and Clegg D (1965) Teaching Drama. London: ULP.

Piaget J (1955) The Child's Construction of Reality. London: Routledge and Kegan Paul.

Pilgrim D (1997) Psychotherapy and Society. London: Sage.

Pilgrim D and Hitchman L (1999) User involvement in mental health service development. In This is Madness. Ross-on-Wye: PCCS Books.

Pines M (1993) The Evolution of Group Analysis. London: Routledge.

Portmann–Tselikas E (Ed) (1999) in Supervision and Dramatherapy. London: Jessica Kingsley.

Proctor B (2000) Group Supervision: A Guide to Creative Practice. London: Sage.

Rapp H (1999) Taking Supervision Forward. Lawton and Feltham Eds. pp 93–112. London: Sage.

Renton G (1981) Unpublished seminar paper.

Rigg R (1998) On becoming a counsellor. Changes Vol 16. No 2. p 131.

Rioch MJ (1980) Supervision. Dilemmas of supervision in dynamic psychotherapy. In AK Hess (Ed) Psychotherapy Supervision: Therapy, Research and Practice. New York: Wiley.

Rogers C (1967) On Becoming a Person. London: Constable.

Rowan J (1995) in: Becoming a Supervisor. Part 2. Inskipp and Proctor. Cascade: Twickenham.

Scott J (2000) Dissociative Identity Disorder. Changes Vol 18. No 1. p 6.

Sharpe M (Ed) (1995) The Third Eye: Supervision of Analytic Groups. London: Routledge.

Slade P (1954) Child Drama. London: ULP.

Stoltenberg CD and Delworth U (1987) Supervising Counsellors and Therapists. San Francisco: Jossey-Bass.

Storr A (1972) The Art of Psychotherapy. London: Secker & Warburg.

Strozier AL (1993) Supervisor intentions, supervisee reactions etc. a case study. Journal: Theory, Research and Practice. Vol 24. pp 13-19.

Sutherland S (1976) Breakdown. London: Weidenfeld and Nicholson.

Szecsody I (1990) Psychoanalytic Psychotherapy. Vol 4. No 3. pp 245-261.

Vernon MD (1971) The Psychology of Perception. Harmondsworth: Penguin Books.

Warren MA and Fox L (1999) in Supervision and Dramatherapy. Tselikas-Portmann E (Ed). pp 220-225. London: Jessica Kingsley.

Way B (1967) Development through Drama. London: Humanity Press.

Webb A (1999) The difficulty of speaking. In Taking Supervision Forward, Lawton and Feltham (Eds) London: Sage.

West W (1999) Supervision difficulties and dilemmas for counsellors and psychotherapists whose work involves healing and spirituality. In Taking Supervision Forward. Eds. Lawton and Feltham. London: Sage.

Wharam T (1992) The building blocks of dramatherapy. Dramatherapy Theory and Practice 2. S Jennings (Ed.) London: Tavistock/Routledge.

Winnicott DW (1974) Playing and Reality. Harmondsworth: Penguin.

Wolff HH (1966) Group dynamics in a supervisory group of students learning psychotherapy, in: The International Handbook of Group Psychotherapy ed. JL Moreno. London: Peter Owen.

Yalom I (1975) The Theory and Practice of Group Psychotherapy. New York: Basic Books.

Zinkin L (1995) Supervision: the impossible profession in Kugler, P. (Ed.) Jungian Perspectives on Supervision, Daimon Verlag: Switzerland.

# Index